Student Workbook
to accompany

Introduction to
Criminal Justice
RESEARCH
AND
STATISTICS

Larry S. Miller
John T. Whitehead
with
Monica Robbers

anderson publishing co.
p.o. box 1576
cincinnati, oh 45201-1576
(513) 421-4142

Student Workbook to Accompany
Introduction to Criminal Justice Research and Statistics

ISBN 0-87084-612-4

 The text of this book is printed on recycled paper.

Ellen S. Boyne *Editor*

Kelly Grondin *Managing Editor*

Cover design by Edward Smith Design, Inc.

Preface

This student workbook is intended to help students understand and master the concepts and issues presented in our text, *Introduction to Criminal Justice Research and Statistics*. Each chapter in this workbook contains a list of key terms and names, a chapter summary and various questions about the important terms and concepts in the text. In the back of this book, there is an appendix with case study problems as well as a handy pull-out math review. The review, like all of the pages in this workbook, is printed on perforated paper that can be removed easily. We think that if you study the chapter in the text, study the workbook and complete the answers in it, you should do well in the course.

We suggest that you proceed in the following order:

1. Look at the workbook, especially the list of key terms.

2. Read the chapter in the text.

3. Make notes and underline important points in your text.

4. Read the chapter summary in the workbook. Make notes and underline important points.

5. Try to answer the questions.

At examination time, reread the chapter in the text and study all of your notes and underlinings in the text and in the workbook summary, and then review the questions in the guide. If you follow these suggestions, you should be well prepared for examination questions.

This student workbook is the product of many individuals. Graduate assistants Michele Slocum and Anessa Zinn wrote drafts of key terms and questions for each chapter. Graduate assistant Monica Robbers wrote draft chapter summaries and fill-in-the blank questions. Next, the material was edited and new material (especially additional questions) was added to each chapter in the workbook. The result is that both graduate students and ourselves had an opportunity to look at the text and point out the important materials and draft questions. We hope that this workbook will be of assistance to you as you study criminal justice research and statistics. As we wrote in the preface to the text, we realize that research methods and statistics can cause undue anxiety. We offer this student workbook to help allay as much of that anxiety as possible.

We thank Michele, Anessa, and Monica for their hard work on this project. We are also grateful to everyone at Anderson Publishing Co. for their sponsorship of our text. Ellen Boyne did a superb job of editing the text. In particular, we thank Mickey Braswell for supporting this project and for his helpful suggestions for the book.

LSM
JTW

Contents

1   The Scientific Method

KEY TERMS AND NAMES

evaluation research
falsifiable
field observation
intuitive-artistic knowledge
logical reasoning
participant observation
qualitative research
quantitative research

research methods
revelation
scientific knowledge
sociological information
statistics
survey research
testable

Carl Klockars
James Marquart

CHAPTER SUMMARY

I. Introduction

A. Statistics is a formal way of making decisions. Statistics is not impossible!

B. The study of statistics is needed to make more informed decisions in the criminal justice system. Findings from research are especially important so we make more informed decisions. For example, research conducted in Kansas City indicated that putting more patrol cars on the roads was not going to decrease crime. Studies of response time showed that citizens often delay in calling the police and thus suspects tend to flee the scene of the crime by the time the police are called. Thus, researching a topic can save time and resources in the long run.

II. Ways of Knowing

A. *Revelation:* Revelation is communication, usually passed down through generations, that is believed to have come from a deity of some sort. One problem is that each generation interprets the information differently.

B. *Intuitive-artistic knowledge:* Intuitive-artistic knowledge is the ability to communicate insights through language and other forms (e.g., literature and painting). An artist can "see" facets of life that the ordinary person does not.

C. *Logical reasoning:* Logical reasoning is comprised of rational arguments used to determine a decision. (Some things are self-evident and do not require explanation.)

III. The Nature and Limits of Scientific Knowledge

Scientific knowledge is based on observations that are: (1) measurable, (2) testable, and (3) falsifiable (i.e., scientists agree on the conditions under which a statement is not true).

A. *Clarifying examples:* For example, the statement "does God exist?" cannot be measured and there is no test that would satisfy everyone that God does exist, so it is more a matter of opinion. The statement cannot be empirically tested. Because it cannot be proved or disproved, it is not a scientific statement.

B. For the purposes of social scientists such as criminologists, testing relationships between variables is more frequent than philosophizing about theories at a highly abstract level.

IV. Some Broader Issues

A. *Free will:* Scientists are moving away from the rigid limits of scientific knowledge to broader perspectives that include concepts such as self-influence. An example of the study of free will is the notion of personal responsibility now being included in some theoretical studies of delinquency.

B. *The relationship between science and policy:* Science and policy are closely intertwined. Many social scientists are funded through such agencies as the National Institute of Justice. Whatever policies or concerns are being adopted by the current government are generally the research subjects that will be funded. For example, in 1991 Ralph Weisheit conducted a funded study of marijuana growers in Illinois in concurrence with the Bush administration's policy on drug addiction. The research was funded in the hope that it might contribute to the war on drugs.

C. *Further example:* C. Wright Mills raises the point that it makes little sense for social scientists to study events in a broad and historical context as opposed to looking only at personal circumstance. For example, with regard to a divorce, instead of blaming the parties' personal problems, a scientist would look to social pressures such as careers and the strains they put on a marriage.

Petersilia criticizes criminologists for concentrating on "pure research" and advocates research that can actually be implemented.

V. Examples of Criminological Research

A. Carl Klockars's study of a professional fence involved in-depth interviewing and observations to learn about the rationalizations for illegal activity.

B. James Marquart's participant observation study of prison guards in Texas enabled him to witness guard brutality and obtain a detailed understanding of guard mentality. A different type of study would not have allowed this valuable insight. (Marquart's study is discussed in more detail in chapter 17). Both Klockars's and Marquart's studies are examples of qualitative studies, which means that they are based on trying to understand the subjective experiences of the subjects in as complete a manner as possible.

C. *Survey research:* Survey research is usually done by questionnaires through the mail or other means. Travis Hirschi surveyed 5,000 students about delinquent acts they had committed. He analyzed his research from an empirical standpoint, which led him to a discussion of why some people are more prone to delinquent behavior than others, thus adding a sociological theory. John Whitehead's study of burnout and job satisfaction in probation officers revealed that most officers are satisfied with their jobs. Both of these surveys are examples of *quantitative* research because their results could be analyzed statistically.

D. *Evaluation research:* Petersilia and Turner conducted a study of special intensive strategies used in probation. They concluded that intensive probation strategies did not decrease recidivism rates.

VI. Research Methodology and Scientific Theory

Although the method of research is important, without a theoretical perspective, a criminological study or any scientific study is not complete. Methodology builds on theory.

EXERCISES

Fill-in-the-Blank Questions

1. The passing on of information from one generation to the next is called _____.

2. Artist's impressions are examples of _____ _____.

3. Scientific knowledge is based on observations that are measurable, _____ and _____.

4. Qualitative research is based on _____ _____ of the participants.

5. An example of quantitative research was carried out by _____ _____, who did a survey on delinquency.

6. Research that has results that can be analyzed statistically is called _____ research.

7. Without _____ research cannot be complete.

Multiple-Choice Questions

_____ 1. Which of the following is true concerning courses in statistics and research methods?

    a. There may be some anxiety associated with such courses
    b. Such courses may not be as appealing as elective courses
    c. Statistics can be difficult but regular study can help assure a passing grade
    d. all of the above

_____ 2. What will probably be the major advantage of this course?

    a. It will assist you to be a more informed student of criminal justice
    b. It will help you to graduate
    c. It will give you something to do at this time everyday
    d. all of the above

_____ 3. The Kansas City Preventive Patrol Experiment tested varying levels of car patrol in Kansas City and found that:

    a. increased car patrol decreased crime
    b. decreased car patrol increased crime
    c. various levels of car patrol had little or no impact on crime levels
    d. foot patrol is more effective than car patrol

_____ 4. What are the nonscientific ways of knowing?

    a. revelation
    b. artistic knowledge
    c. logic
    d. all of the above

_____ 5. Revelatory knowledge entails:

    a. a belief that a deity has communicated certain truths to humans
    b. having a gift of "seeing" aspects of life that many of us fail to see because we are so busy
    c. observations that are measurable, testable and falsifiable
    d. abstract philosophical reasoning

_____ 6. Scientific knowledge entails:

    a. a belief that a deity has communicated certain truths to humans
    b. having a gift of "seeing" aspects of life that many of us fail to see because we are so busy
    c. observations that are measurable, testable and falsifiable
    d. abstract philosophical reasoning

_____ 7. Logical reasoning is based on:

    a. the assumption that God exists
    b. the idea that certain truths are self-evident or must be assumed to be true for human activity to go on
    c. the notion that human suffering will be rewarded in the hereafter
    d. none of the above

_____ 8. Which of the following is *not* a characteristic of scientific knowledge?

    a. measurable
    b. testable
    c. falsifiable
    d. intuitive

_____ 9. Which of the following is a danger of government funding of research by grants?

    a. pressure to pursue topics of interest to lawmakers
    b. pressure to study topics of interest to the community
    c. wasteful studies
    d. all of the above

_____ 10. Qualitative research is characterized by:

    a. the use of advanced statistical procedures
    b. attention to the objective experiences of the subjects
    c. attention to the subjective experiences of the subjects
    d. attention to detail

_____ 11. Which of the following is a quantitative research strategy frequently used by social scientists?

    a. participant observation
    b. field observation
    c. questionnaire survey
    d. ethnomethodology

True/False Questions

_____ 1. Research methods and statistics simply offer formalized ways of gathering information to make better informed decisions.

_____ 2. Research is sometimes conducted simply to gather information rather than to test hypotheses in a formal manner.

_____ 3. Statistics and research methods courses have no contributions to make to persons interested in police operations, the death penalty or correctional interventions.

_____ 4. Taking a statistics course will probably not help you to become a better criminal justice professional.

_____ 5. Research has indicated that increasing the levels of car patrol in a city will probably not have a dramatic impact on the crime rate in that city.

_____ 6. Intuitive-artistic persons have a gift for "seeing" aspects of the world that most of us fail to see because we are so immersed in everyday details.

_____ 7. One characteristic of scientific knowledge is that it is empirical.

_____ 8. That scientific knowledge is testable means that it can be tested only in a laboratory.

_____ 9. "Falsifiable" means that scientists agree on the conditions in which a statement is not true.

_____ 10. Science is not as value-free and culture-free as was once thought.

_____ 11. Quantitative research is automatically more difficult to conduct and analyze than qualitative research.

_____ 12. The ability to see what many think are only personal problems as social problems has been called the sociological prestidigitation.

Essay/Discussion Questions

1. Which of the ways of knowing do you prefer? Why?

_____

_____

_____

_____

_____

_____

_____

_____

_____

_____

_____

_____

_____

_____

_____

2. Discuss a movie or book you have seen/read lately. What message did the movie/book have to offer? How do you think that the filmmaker/author arrived at the message that he or she was trying to convey? How do we assess the validity of an artistic method? Does art necessarily have to have a message?

_____

_____

_____

_____

_____

_____

_____

_____

_____

_____

_____

_____

_____

_____

3. Why might science and religion come into conflict? Is such conflict inevitable? Can it be resolved?

_____
_____
_____
_____
_____
_____
_____
_____
_____
_____
_____
_____
_____
_____
_____
_____

4. What is a scientific question? How do scientific questions differ from nonscientific questions? Can science contribute anything about some of the most important questions in life, such as the meaning of life?

_____
_____
_____
_____
_____
_____
_____
_____
_____
_____
_____
_____
_____
_____

5. The chapter mentions some examples of scientific research. What other examples of scientific research can you mention? For example, have you learned of any recent scientific studies by watching the news or other programs on television? Do any of these recent studies raise any concerns?

_____
_____
_____
_____
_____
_____
_____
_____
_____
_____
_____
_____
_____
_____

6. Are science and art compatible? Can the same individuals be talented scientifically and artistically?

_____
_____
_____
_____
_____
_____
_____
_____
_____
_____
_____
_____
_____
_____

2

The Logic of
Hypothesis Testing

KEY TERMS

alternative research hypothesis	nominal data
causality	null hypothesis (H_o)
concepts	operationalization
continuous quantitative variable	ordinal data
data	qualitative variable
dependent variable	quantitative variable
dichotomous	ratio data
discrete quantitative variable	research hypothesis (H_a)
hypotheses	rival hypothesis
independent variable	scientific research
interval data	spurious relationship
measurement	theory
multinomial	variables

CHAPTER SUMMARY

I. Introduction

A. *Hypothesis:* A hypothesis is a specific, testable statement that shows a relationship between two or more variable (as opposed to a theory, which is a generalized statement about variables). For example, we may theorize that education affects crime rate. The hypothesis could be the higher the level of education, the less likely it is for a person to commit a crime. We are attempting to explain a phenomenon.

B. *Research hypothesis:* The research hypothesis is the hypothesis that the researcher believes to be true. In our example above, we might believe that the more years of education one has, the lower his or her number of prior arrests.

C. *Null hypothesis:* The null hypothesis is a hypothesis of no difference, which means that there is no relationship between the variables. In order to reject the null hypothesis, the researcher must obtain sufficient amounts of evidence to accept the research hypothesis and say that there is a relationship between the variables. The null hypothesis is assumed to be true until it can be disproved.

II. Measurement

The research hypothesis must be measurable numerically. Measurement then can yield data. The first step in deciding how to measure variables is to define the concepts.

A. *Concepts:* Concepts are labels given to variable. They must be operationally defined so that everyone knows what the researcher is specifically discussing.

B. A concept is operational if it is measurable.

C. A variable is a concept that is operationalized. It is a logical grouping of attributes. A variable can have a numerical value such as a test score, or it can have a non-numeric value, such as gender.

D. Measurement of variables:

1. *Qualitative variable:* A qualitative variable is a variable that is not usually measured on a numerical scale. For example, race or gender. Qualitative variables can be dichotomous (two categories, e.g., male, female) or multinominal (many categories, e.g., black, white, Hispanic, etc.).

2. *Quantitative variable:* A quantitative variable is a variable that can be analyzed statistically (e.g., an annual salary). They can be discrete (consisting of counts or frequencies) or continuous (consisting of all possible points on a scale.)

III. Levels of Measurement

Data means different things depending on its sophistication.

A. *Nominal-level data:* Nominal-level data is the simplest level of measurement a variable can assume. There is no statistical or numeric meaning to these variables; they are labels or symbols. Properties are mutually exclusive and exhaustive.

B. *Ordinal-level data:* Ordinal-level data contains all the properties of nominal-level data and also enables the placement of objects into ranks (e.g., highest, next highest, etc.). Exemplifying this type of data are many attitudinal scales used in the social science arena.

C. *Interval-level data:* Internal-level data contains all the elements of ordinal and nominal data and enables the placement of objects into ranks with equal distance between objects.

D. *Ratio-level data:* Ratio-level data assumes all the qualities of interval data and adds a zero point with meaning (e.g., "zero income" has a definite meaning).

It is important that the researcher defines his or her variables at the highest level of measurement possible.

IV. Independent and Dependent Variables

A. *Independent variable:* The independent variable is a variable that influences the dependent variable or is the cause.

B. *Dependent variable:* The dependent variable is the effect. For example, there is a correlation between gender and GPA. If you are female (the independent variable or cause), your GPA is likely to be higher (the dependent variable or effect.).

V. Causality

A. The relationships between variables can be shown to be causal. To establish causality the following steps must be taken:

    1. Establish a relationship between X (the independent variable) and Y (the dependent variable).

    2. Place X and Y into time order. X must be first; otherwise, the variables are incorrect. In order for X to cause Y, X must precede Y in time.

    3. Make sure there is no third or rival variable (Z). If you find a third variable, you cannot conclude that X causes Y. For example, assume that the speed limit is 55 mph (X) and the accident rate is Y. Y has decreased dramatically from 1960 to 1980, so we can say that the roads are safer. However, technological advances during that time period have led to safer cars, so it is possible that the third variable of safer cars may be affecting the rate (i.e., causing Y).

B. *Spurious relationships:* Spurious relationships are relationships that occur when variables X and Y are related only because they are affected by a third variable Z.

EXERCISES

Short-Answer Questions

1. Classify the following variables as (a) qualitative or quantitative, and (b) as dichotomous/multinomial or discrete/continuous:

    a. The number of DUI arrests over one weekend.

    b. The number of police officers attending an in-service training school.

    c. The success rate of probationers not recidivating.

    d. The annual income of correctional counselors.

    e. The races of inmates in prison.

2. Classify the numbers describing each of the following as nominal, ordinal, interval or ratio data:

    a. Makes of sidearms for police officers.

    b. Location of residential burglaries by zone.

    c. Ratings of juvenile treatment programs on a scale from 1 to 10.

    d. The number of juveniles incarcerated in a detention facility over one weekend.

    e. Numerical score on a GED test for inmates in a prison.

    f. IQs of inmates on death row.

    g. Ratings of rookie police officers from "High Performance" to "Low Performance."

    h. Religious preference of prisoners.

    i. Geographic region.

    j. The number of miles traveled by police cruisers during one year.

3. A police training instructor is interested in how effective a new video on self-defense is in training officers. The instructor believes the new video will increase officers' awareness of the need for self-defense tactics. She compares performance scores of officers trained with the new video with the scores of past officers who were not trained with the new video.

    a. Formulate a research hypothesis for this situation:

        H_a:

    b. Formulate a null hypothesis for this situation:

        H_o:

    c. Identify the independent and dependent variables:

        $X =$

        $Y =$

    d. How would the independent and dependent variables be measured?

        $X =$

        $Y =$

Multiple-Choice Questions

_____ 1. To explain criminal behavior, scientists use:

    a. theories
    b. hypotheses
    c. opinions
    d. both a and b

_____ 2. Hypotheses are:

    a. broad statements regarding some phenomena
    b. specific statements derived from theory
    c. statements regarding the relationship between two or more variables
    d. both b and c

_____ 3. The research hypothesis is designated by the symbol:

    a. H_o
    b. H_1
    c. H_a
    d. none of the above

_____ 4. The null hypothesis is designated by the symbol:

    a. H_o
    b. H_1
    c. H_a
    d. none of the above

_____ 5. In scientific research the null hypothesis is:

    a. a statement of nothingness, no difference
    b. is tested
    c. is either rejected in favor of the research hypothesis or it is not rejected
    d. all of the above are correct

_____ 6. In scientific research a hypothesis must be:

    a. easy to understand
    b. measurable
    c. theoretical
    d. none of the above

_____ 7. Measurement can be defined as _____.

    a. the assignment of numbers to characteristics that are being observed
    b. abstract labels put on reality
    c. concepts that have been operationalized
    d. all of the above

_____ 8. Concepts:

    a. are abstract labels put on reality
    b. must be defined so that everyone knows what the researcher is talking about
    c. include crime, delinquency and intelligence
    d. all of the above

_____ 9. A qualitative variable:

    a. varies in degree but not in kind
    b. can be either dichotomous or multinomial
    c   varies in kind but not degree
    d. can either be discrete or continuous
    e. b and c are correct

_____ 10. Which of the following could be considered to be a level of measurement?

    a. nominal
    b. ordinal
    c. interval
    d. ratio
    e. all of the above

_____ 11. The independent variable is a variable that:

      a.   is dependent upon some other variable
      b.   can be changed, altered or manipulated by the researcher
      c.   is denoted by the symbol Y
      d.   is the effect

_____ 12. In order to establish causality a scientist must:

      a.   demonstrate a relationship between two or more variables
      b.   specify the independent and dependent variables
      c.   eliminate rival causal factors
      d.   all of the above

True/False Questions

_____ 1. Theories are generally broad statements regarding some phenomena.

_____ 2. Hypotheses are more general statements derived from theory.

_____ 3. A research hypothesis is a statement the researcher believes to be true.

_____ 4. The null hypothesis is a statement of no relationship.

_____ 5. In scientific research the research hypothesis is the one that is tested.

_____ 6. A null hypothesis can be shown to be true.

_____ 7. Measurement yields data.

_____ 8. Variables are concepts that have been operationalized.

_____ 9. A qualitative variable is one that varies in degree but not in kind.

_____ 10. Quantitative variables can be either discrete or continuous.

_____ 11. Interval data is the only level of measurement that has an absolute zero point.

_____ 12. When one variable is manipulated by a researcher, and this causes an effect in the other variable, that is referred to as a relationship.

_____ 13. The dependent variable is denoted by the symbol Y.

_____ 14. Nominal data suggests an implied order.

Essay/Discussion Questions

1. Explain the levels of measurement. Give examples of each level.

2. Explain how the null hypothesis differs from the research hypothesis. Which is more important? Why?

3.   What does causality mean in scientific terms?

_____

_____

_____

_____

_____

_____

_____

_____

_____

_____

4.   Identify a problem that you see with police practices in your community. Explain the problem by outlining a short theory and hypothesis. Operationalize your hypothesis by identifying the independent and dependent variables and explain the level of measurement for each.

_____

_____

_____

_____

_____

_____

_____

_____

_____

_____

_____

_____

_____

_____

_____

_____

_____

_____

3 Descriptive Statistics

KEY TERMS

bar graph
column percents
contingency tables
crosstabulations
cumulative frequency
cumulative percent
descriptive statistics
exhaustive
frequency distribution
frequency polygon
graphs
grouped frequency distribution
index crimes
inferential statistics
line chart

mutually exclusive
ogive
ordered array
percent
pie chart
proportions
rates
ratios
row percents
statistics
stem-and-leaf diagram
Sturgess's Rule
total percents
UCR

CHAPTER SUMMARY

I. Descriptive Statistics

Descriptive statistics are techniques that summarize a large amount of numerical information. Examples of such techniques include graphs, frequency distributions and tables. *Inferential statistics* are statistics that allow us to make an inference about an entire population even though we do not have access to it. Inferential statistics include Pearson's *r* correlation coefficient, chi-square and regression coefficients. The specifics of inferential statistics are covered in later chapters.

II. Percents, Proportions, Rates and Ratios

These are all useful in comparing populations.

A. *Percent:* the frequency of an event divided by the total and multiplied by 100.

$$\frac{\text{frequency of event}}{\text{total}} \times 100$$

For example, let us say there are 22 female inmates on death row in California in a prison population of 600. What is the percentage of female inmates?

$$\frac{22}{600} \times 100$$
$$= 0.0367 \times 100$$
$$= 3.67\%$$

Therefore, 3.67% of the inmates at this California prison are females.

B. *Proportion:* the frequency of an event divided by the total.

$$\frac{\text{frequency of event}}{\text{total}}$$

For example, if we wanted to know the proportion of female prisoners in the above example:

$$\frac{22}{600} = 0.367.$$

C. *Rate:* a proportion based on some population.
For a population of 100,000,

$$\text{rate} = \frac{\text{number of events}}{\text{potential number}} \times 100,000$$

If we look at the female prisoners example, our proportion of 0.0367 is difficult to comprehend, but if we use a rate, the rate of female prisoners in the California prison is:

$$\frac{22}{600} \times 100,000$$
$$= 0.0367 \times 100,000$$
$$= 3,670$$

Therefore, in every 100,000 prison inmates on death row, 3,670 of them will be females.

(Note: Victimization rates are usually calculated using a population of 1,000 instead of 100,000.)

D. *Ratio:* the frequency of event 1 divided by the frequency of event 2.

$$\text{ratio} = \frac{\text{frequency of event one}}{\text{frequency of event two}}$$

The ratio of male to female prisoners is

$$\frac{600}{22}$$

$$= 27.27$$

Therefore, for every one female prisoner, there are 27 male prisoners.

III. Frequency Distribution

Frequency distributions are methods by which large amounts of data are displayed by the frequency with which they occur. These can be used for data of all levels of measurement (nominal, ordinal, interval, ratio). A frequency distribution usually has two columns, the left column displaying the name of the variables and the right column displaying the frequency.

Consider a group of data like this:
1, 1, 1, 2, 2, 2, 3, 4

We would set up a frequency table like this:

No.(x)	f
1	3
2	3
3	1
4	1
	$n = 8$

Where: x = the score
f = frequency
n = total number of scores

IV. Grouped Frequency Distribution

Quantitative variables that have many scores and high frequencies are better displayed as grouped frequency distributions. The researcher must decide how to group the data. (A suggestion is to include between five and 20 classes.)

A. Sturgess's Rule—helps the researcher decide how many groups to use:

$$\text{Approx. class width} = \frac{\text{largest value - smallest value in data set}}{\text{desired number of classes}}$$

grade	f	grade	f	grade	f	grade	f
99	0	85	2	71	4	57	0
98	1	84	1	70	9	56	1
97	0	83	0	69	3	55	0
96	1	82	3	68	5	54	1
95	1	81	1	67	1	53	0
94	1	80	2	66	3	52	1
93	0	79	8	65	0	51	1
92	1	78	1	64	1	50	1
91	1	77	0	63	2		
90	0	76	2	62	0		
89	1	75	1	61	0		
88	0	74	1	60	2		
87	1	73	1	59	3		
86	0	72	2	58	1		

$n = 71$

First, subtract the smallest score from the largest score in the data set (99 - 50 = 49). Next, divide by the desired number of classes (49/10 = 4.9) and round it off (5). The groups must then be exhaustive (covering the entire range of data) and mutually exclusive (*not* overlapping).

Grouped Frequency Distribution of Final Examination Grades for 71 Students

class interval	f	%	cf	c%
95-99	3	4.23	3	4.23
90-94	2	2.82	5	7.05
85-89	4	5.63	9	12.68
80-84	7	9.86	16	22.54
75-79	12	16.90	28	39.44
70-74	17	23.94	45	63.38
65-69	12	16.90	57	80.28
60-64	5	7.04	62	87.32
55-59	5	7.04	67	94.36
50-54	4	5.63	71	99.99
total	71	100	71	100

Included in this table is a cumulative frequency (*cf*) column and a cumulative percent (*c*%) column. Cumulative frequencies are computed and each successive percent is added on. Cumulations make frequency tables easier to read.

V. Crosstabulation

Crosstabulations allow the researcher to look at two frequency distributions at the same time.

The independent variable, rather than the dependent variable, is percentaged as 100 percent. This helps to establish causation. If it is difficult to determine which variable is which, use total percents in the crosstabulation. Then, instead of looking for a causal relationship, we can merely determine whether a relationship exists.

VI. Graphs

Graphs present a clear picture of statistics.

A. *Pie-charts:* Pie charts are circular graphs comprised of pie-shaped "pieces" that when added together equal 100 percent.

B. *Bar graphs and line graphs:* (1) Bar graphs are also referred to as *histograms.* A bar graph is a set of bars on an axis; the horizontal axis represents x (the measured variable) and the vertical axis represents f (frequency). (2) Line graphs, also called *frequency polygons,* follow the same format except that instead of bars, the points are plotted and then connected with a straight line.

C. *Ogives:* Ogives are graphs in which cumulative frequencies are placed on the vertical axis.

D. *Stem-and-leaf diagrams:* Stem-and-leaf diagrams are diagrams that combine the features of an ordered array of numbers and a histogram. The following is an example with 20 tests scores ranging from 98 to 70:

Stem	Leaf	Frequency
9	02688	5
8	001224788	9
7	022458	6

VII. Uniform Crime Reports

The U.S. Department of Justice compiles the Uniform Crime Reports (UCR) from information collected from each state. Although they are often used by the media to illustrate trends, these statistics are not completely accurate because they contain only those crimes that are known to the police.

The UCR is divided into two sections. Part One includes *index crimes,* which are serious crimes such as manslaughter, rape and robbery. Part Two contains nonindex crimes such as public drunkenness, simple assault, etc.

VIII. Bureau of Justice Statistics

The Bureau of Justice Statistics (BJS) is an agency of the Department of Justice that publishes data and reports of descriptive criminal justice statistics. The BJS also publishes the Sourcebook of Criminal Justice Statistics, which contains statistical information about prisoners, parole, offense frequency, and other criminal justice topics.

EXERCISES

Short-Answer Questions

1. If city A has 400 reported crimes and a population of 15,000, and city B has 250 reported crimes and a population of 900,000,

    a)   what is the crime rate in city A?

    b)   what is the crime rate in city B?

    c)   what is the ratio of crime in city A compared to city B ?

2. The following crimes were reported on the university campus in the month of January, rape—1, assault (simple)—7, evading arrest—2, larceny—1, speeding—25, theft—8, alcohol violations—16.

    Construct a cumulative frequency table and include percentages and cumulative percentages for this data. What is the percent of alcohol violations of reported crimes in January?

3. Homicide and aggravated assault are examples of _____ crimes.

4. The following test scores were collected from several different criminology classes:

Whitehead		Haas		Miller	
94	80	55	62	90	88
96	83	70	78	92	86
98	64	38	82	94	87
84	72	42	99	99	74
83	77	92	78	100	72
82	90	86	64	64	55
78	55	67	51	71	55
76	41	82	58	76	100
74	63	82	49	91	84
50	86	83	53	63	90
53	88	53	93	80	89

Combine all the scores and construct a grouped frequency distribution. Include percentages.

Multiple-Choice Questions

_____ 1. Numbers or measurements that summarize events are called:

      a. graphs
      b. charts
      c. statistics
      d. tables

_____ 2. The discipline that obtains, organizes, summarizes, presents and/or analyzes numerical facts is called:

      a. statistics
      b. numerology
      c. astrology
      d. chartology

_____ 3. Which of the following summarizes large volumes of numerical information?

      a. statistics
      b. inferential statistics
      c. descriptive statistics
      d. contingency tables

_____ 4. Sets of procedures that allow us to reach conclusions about some population are called:

      a. tables
      b. descriptive statistics
      c. inferential statistics
      d. charts

_____ 5. With _____, we can observe trends; define percentages, proportions and rates of given variables; and prepare graphs and other pictorial representations.

      a. inferential statistics
      b. statistics
      c. descriptive statistics
      d. charts

_____ 6. The frequency of an event divided by the total number multiplied by 100 is the:

      a. percent
      b. proportion
      c. rate
      d. ratio

_____ 7. The frequency of an event divided by the total number and expressed in decimal form is the:

      a. percent
      b. proportion
      c. rate
      d. ratio

_____ 8. The number of events divided by the total number at risk and multiplied by 100,000 is the:

    a. percent
    b. proportion
    c. rate
    d. ratio

_____ 9. Victimizations rates are calculated as rates per _____ persons at risk.

    a. 1,000
    b. 10,000
    c. 100,000
    d. 1 million

_____ 10. The frequency of event 1 divided by frequency of event 2 is the:

    a. percent
    b. proportion
    c. rate
    d. ratio

_____ 11. The method by which large sets of data can be divided and displayed in easily readable form is called a:

    a. table
    b. contingency table
    c. percent
    d. frequency distribution

_____ 12. Arranging a set of numbers is called _____.

    a. ascension
    d. descension
    c. ordered array
    d. descending array

_____ 13. The rule that helps the researcher to determine groups in a frequency distribution is:

    a. Sturgill's
    b. Sturgess's
    c. Sturrett's
    d. Sturnett's

_____ 14. In a frequency distribution, class intervals must be _____.

    a. mutually exclusive
    b. exhaustive
    c. both
    d. neither

_____ 15. In a frequency distribution the running total is:

    a. exhaustive
    b. the cumulative percent
    c. mutually exclusive
    d. the cumulative frequency

_____ 16. An examination of two frequency distributions at the same time is called a:

    a. cumulative frequency distribution
    b. cumulative percent
    c. grouped frequency distribution
    d. crosstabulation

_____ 17. One should always use _____ based on the _____ variable when drawing conclusions about causal relationships.

    a. percents, independent
    b. percents, dependent
    c. proportions, independent
    d. proportions, dependent

_____ 18. A circular graph is referred to as a _____.

    a. histogram
    b. frequency polygon
    c. pie chart
    d. bar graph

_____ 19. A cumulative frequency distribution is graphically displayed as a(n) _____.

    a. histogram
    b. ogive
    c. pie chart
    d. stem-and-leaf diagram

_____ 20. The most well-known source of criminal justice descriptive statistics is _____.

    a. Sturgess's Rule
    b. Part 2
    c. the UCR
    d. index offenses

True/False Questions

_____ 1. Inferential statistics are statistics that have to estimated or guessed at.

_____ 2. Descriptive statistics allow one to summarize large amounts of information.

_____ 3. Some well-known examples of descriptive statistics are the mean, the median and the mode.

_____ 4. Inferential statistics allow the researcher to make claims about the population of interest.

_____ 5. The Uniform Crime Reports are divided into three main parts.

_____ 6. Selling a million dollars' worth of heroin would be a Part I or Index Crime.

_____ 7. An ogive is a pie chart.

Essay/Discussion Questions

1. When drawing conclusions on causal relationships based on percents, which variable is best to use, the independent or the dependent? Why?

_____

2. What is the difference between descriptive statistics and inferential statistics?

_____

3.   Which is the better way to display data, using tables or graphs? Why?

4.   What are the Uniform Crime Reports? What kinds of data do they contain? What kinds of studies might one be able to conduct using the UCR?

4

Summary Measures

KEY TERMS

bimodal	mode
fractile	peakedness
interfractile range	percentiles
interpolated	platykurtic
interquartile range	population variance
kurtosis	quartile
leptokurtic	range
lower limit	skewness
mean	standard deviance
measures of central tendency	statistic formula
measures of shape	symmetry
measures of variability	univariate analysis
median	upper limit
mesokurtic	variance
midpoint	

CHAPTER SUMMARY

I. Measures of Central Tendency

These describe the typical scores in a data set.

A. *Mode:* The mode is the most frequently occurring value in a data set. The mode can be used for data at all levels of measurement (nominal, ordinal, interval and ratio).

B. *Median:* The median is the middle value. The median is good for ordinal, interval and ratio data because data must be ranked. To obtain the median, first put all the numbers in ranked order, then find the middle score:

If there is an odd number of scores, the formula is: $n / 2$.

If there is an even number of scores, the formula is: $(n + 1) / 2$.

C. *Mean:* The mean is the average of a group of scores. The mean can be computed only from interval or ratio data. It is calculated by adding the scores or values and dividing by the number of score or values (n). For example, in a survey of IQ scores, the following scores were recorded:

respondents	IQ
A	125
B	92
C	72
D	126
E	120
F	99
G	130
H	100
$n = 8$	864

The mean is: $864 / 8 = 108$.

The mean (or average) of these IQ scores is 108.

Calculating the mean from a frequency table is more complicated. Including a *fx* column makes this much easier:

x	f	fx
8	2	16
7	3	21
6	5	30
5	6	30
4	4	16
3	4	12
2	3	6
1	1	1
$n = 28$		$\Sigma fx = 132$

The mean is: $132 / 28 = 4.71$.

II. Central Tendencies with Grouped Data

The first step to finding measures of central tendencies with grouped data is finding the midpoints of each interval group.

The following is a grouped frequency distribution:

class interval	f
95-99	3
90-94	2
85-89	4
80-84	12
75-79	17
70-74	12

$$\Sigma f = 50$$

A. *Determining the mode in a grouped frequency:* To determine the mode, find the most frequently occurring class interval and calculate its midpoint. For the above example, the interval 75-79 occurs the most often (17 times). To calculate the midpoint, add the interval parameters and divide by two:

75 + 79 / 2 = 77.

Thus the mode is 77.

B. *Determining the mean in a grouped frequency:* To determine the mean for a grouped frequency distribution, the formula.

$$\Sigma fm / n$$

(Σ = sum, m = midpoint, and n = total number of frequencies)

In the above distribution we would add a column for midpoints and a column for frequency multiplied by the midpoint:

class interval	f	m	fm	cf
95-99	3	97	291	50
90-94	2	92	184	47
85-89	4	87	348	45
80-84	12	82	984	41
75-79	17	77	1,309	29
70-74	12	72	864	12

$$\Sigma f = 50 \qquad \Sigma fm = 4,328$$

Mean = 4,328 / 50 = 86.56.

C. *Determining the median in a grouped frequency:* To find the median in a grouped frequency distribution we add a cumulative frequency column. (see above). Then we find the median score in the above example we have 50 scores so the median score is the 25th which lies in the 75-79 interval. To find the exact value of the median we then use the following formula:

$$Md = \text{lower limit of Md interval} + \frac{\frac{N}{2} - \text{cf below the lower limit Md interval}}{f \text{ in Md interval}} \times \text{size of interval}$$

Next, multiply this by the size of the interval.

In our example:

$$74.5 + \frac{50/2 - 12}{17} \times 5$$

$$= 74.5 + \frac{13}{17} \times 5$$

$$= 78.32$$

The lower limit of the critical or median interval is the number just above the next lowest score. Thus, 74.5 is just above 74. The lower limit of the interval 85-89 would be 84.5.

III. Percentiles

These are useful as summary measures to describe data sets. The median is the 50th percentile. A percentile is a value that exceeds a given percentage of the set of data values. For example, the 75th percentile is the value in a data set that has 75 percent of the data below it. If we look at our data set:

interval	f	cf
95-99	3	50
90-99	2	47
85-89	4	45
80-84	12	41
75-79	17	29
70-74	12	12
	$n = 50$	

To find the 75th percentile multiply the total cumulative frequency by 0.75. So, 50 x 0.75 = 37.5. Move up the cumulative frequency column until we find the data value that has 37.5 in it (in this example, it is included in the 80-84 interval because that interval includes the 29th through the 41st value).

IV. Measures of Variability

Central tendency measures do not always give the whole picture of an interval or ratio distribution, so we use variance or spread. Variance can be calculated in two different ways: (1) the distance from a central value (i.e., the mean) or (2) the distances between selected observations.

A. *The range:* The range is the difference between the highest and lowest score in a set of data. If all the data values in a set are the same, then the range is zero. Otherwise:

range = highest value – lowest value

The range is not a very stable measure because if one value is considerably higher than all the others, this will affect the range value. If the range is large, then the distribution has high variability. If the range is small, then the distribution has low variability.

B. *Interfractile ranges:* Interfractile ranges measure the distances between fractiles or percentiles. The most popular interfractile measure is the interfractile or interquartile range. This is the difference between the third (75th) and the first (25th) percentiles. For example, we have a simple frequency distribution:

x	f	cf
7	1	16
6	2	15
5	3	13
4	5	10
3	2	5
2	2	3
1	1	1

$$n = 16$$

The 75th percentile is 0.75 x 16 = 12, located in the score of 5. The 25th percentile is 0.25 x 16 = 4, located in the score of 3. The interquartile range is then 5 – 3 = 2.

Always remember that a single score can distort this measure.

V. The Variance

The variance is the squares of the individual score deviations. Variance is calculated by the following formulas:

For a population (when the mean of the population is given as μ):

$$\sigma^2 \;=\; \frac{\Sigma(X - \mu)^2}{N}$$

For a sample (when the mean is $\overline{X}$):

$$s^2 \;=\; \frac{\Sigma(X - \overline{X})^2}{n - 1}$$

Where: N = size of the population
n = size of sample

To find the variance, first compute the mean.

The formula for the mean is:

$$\overline{X} \;=\; \frac{\Sigma fX}{N}$$

The first column is the value of x. The second column is the value of x minus the mean. The third column is the absolute value of x minus the mean. The fourth column is this absolute value squared. The last column is the x value squared. Be sure to total all columns.

x	$x - \bar{X}$	$(x - \bar{X})$	$(x - \bar{X})^2$	x^2
9	9 - 5 = 4	4	16	81
8	8 - 5 = 3	3	9	64
6	6 - 5 = 1	1	1	36
4	4 - 5 = -1	1	1	16
2	2 - 5 = -3	3	9	4
1	1 - 5 = -4	4	16	1
$\Sigma x = 30$	$\Sigma = 0$	16	52	202

Then we "plug in" the values for our formulas:

Mean = 30 / 6 = 5

Variance = 52 / 6 = 8.67

(Note: Assume that we are dealing with a population and not a sample.)

Standard deviations show how much a score varies from the mean. Most often we will want to work with the standard deviation because the variance is difficult to understand. To find the standard deviation, simply take the square root of the variance (2.94). This means that on the average, scores deviate 2.94 points from the mean (a small standard deviation like this one means that the mean is precise because all the scores are close together).

If a score lies at one deviation from the mean in our above example, this would mean the score has a value of 7.94 because our mean is 5 and our standard deviation is 2.94. If the score lies two standard deviations below the mean, then the score has a value of:

5 - (2 x 2.94) = -0.88

We can also calculate how many scores lie between, for instance, one and three standard deviations from the mean. For example, one standard deviation from the mean is:

5 + 2.94 = 7.94 and 5 + (3 x 2.94) = 13.82

Then we take our scores and count how many lie between 7.94 and 13.82. There are two scores that lie between the first and third standard deviations.

To avoid computing errors when calculating standard deviation and variance, the following formula can be used:

Variance (for raw scores):

$$\sigma^2 = \frac{\Sigma x^2}{N} - \bar{X}^2$$

Variance (in a frequency distribution):

$$\sigma^2 = \frac{\Sigma f(X^2)}{N} - \bar{X}^2$$

The formula for variance in a frequency distribution involves setting up a total of five columns. The first lists the x value. The second column displays the frequency. The third column displays the frequency multiplied by x. The fourth column displays x squared. The fifth column displays fx squared.

VI. Determining the Variance and Standard Deviation with Grouped Data

To find the variance and standard deviation of grouped data, we use the midpoints of each class interval. Using the following set of data, first calculate the midpoint, then multiply the midpoint by the frequency. Then, square this value. We also have to find the mean of the data set. The formula for grouped data sets is given in the previous section (Section II).

class interval	f	m	fm	$f(m^2)$
17-19	1	18	18	324
14-16	2	15	30	450
11-13	3	12	36	432
8-10	5	9	45	405
5-7	4	6	24	144
2-4	2	3	6	18
	$n = 17$		159	1,773

Variance:

$$\sigma^2 = \frac{\Sigma f(m^2)}{N} - \overline{X}^2$$

Plug in the values:

$$\text{Variance} = \frac{1,773}{17} - (9.35)^2$$

$$= 104.29 - 87.42$$

$$= 16.87$$

The standard deviation is the square root of this final figure (16.87): 4.11.

Note: For use in all examples, rounding to the nearest tenth is adequate. You may want to round to the nearest hundredth for more accurate results.

VII. Measures of Shape

Every frequency level distribution takes on a particular shape. When we plot points of such a distribution and connect the points with a line, usually the distribution will take on a bell shape. We can describe the distribution based on its shape.

A. *Skewness*: Skewness is the degree of asymmetry evident in a distribution's curve. If the shape of a distribution has symmetrical shape, that is, one half mirrors the other half, then the bell-shaped normal curve possesses no skewness. If the distribution has a long tail on the right, then the distribution is considered to be skewed to the right (positively skewed). If the distribution has a long tail to the left, it is skewed to the left (negatively skewed). In a symmetrical curve, the median, mode and mean all lie at the same location. If the distribution is skewed to the left, a few extreme values lie below the mean. If the distribution is skewed to the right, then a few extreme values lie above the mean.

B. *Measure of Skewness*: The amount of skewness can be calculated using the following formula:

$$\text{coefficient of skewness} = \frac{3(\overline{X} - Md)}{\sigma}$$

Where: $\overline{X}$ = mean
Md = median
σ = standard deviation

The coefficient of skewness will always be less than one. The larger the number, the greater the amount of skewness. Whether the number is positive or negative will determine in which direction the curve is skewed.

C. *Frequency curves*: Frequency curves also can be described on the basis of their shape. *Mesokurtic* is a moderate peak, *leptokurtic* is a sharp peak, and *platykurtic* is a flat curve.

Exercise

EXERCISES

Short-Answer Questions

Answer the questions from the following grouped frequency distribution.

interval	frequency
41-45	23
46-50	5
51-55	7
56-60	12
61-65	8
66-70	5
71-75	14
76-80	1

a. Find the mode.

b. Find the median.

c. Find the mean.

d. What is the standard deviation for this distribution?

e. What is the variance for this distribution?

f. What percentage of scores lie above the 75th percentile?

g. How many scores lie between the 25th and 50th percentile?

h. What percent of scores fall between +1 and -1 standard deviations?

i. What percent of scores fall between +1 and +2 standard deviations?

j. Describe the symmetry of the distribution using the skewness coefficient.

Multiple-Choice Questions

_____ 1. Data of a single variable can be summarized three ways. Which of the following is not one of them?

   a. measure of central tendency
   b. measure of variability
   c. measure of shape
   d. measure of reliability

_____ 2. Which of the following is/are measure(s) of central tendency?

   a. mean
   b. median
   c. mode
   d. all of the above

_____ 3. The most frequently occurring value or score in a set of data is the _____.

   a. mean
   b. median
   c. mode
   d. standard deviation

_____ 4. The 50th percentile is also known as the:

   a. median
   b. mode
   c. mean
   d. standard deviation

_____ 5. The most frequently used measure of central tendency is the:

   a. median
   b. mean
   c. mode
   d. percentile

_____ 6. To determine central tendency in grouped data, you must find the _____.

   a. mean
   b. median
   c. frequency
   d. midpoint

_____ 7. If the measured variable is ordinal, which measure of central tendency could be used?

   a. median
   b. mode
   c. both
   d. neither

_____ 8. Which measure of central tendency can be used with nominal data?

   a. mean
   b. median
   c. mode
   d. percentile

_____ 9. The statistic that exceeds a given percentage of a set of data values is a _____.

    a. percentile
    b. mean
    c. mode
    d. fractile

_____ 10. Spread or dispersion in a data set is defined as _____.

    a. variability
    b. variation
    c. standard deviation
    d. percentile

_____ 11. The difference between the largest and smallest values in the data set is the _____.

    a. range
    b. midpoint
    c. mean
    d. average

_____ 12. The _____ measures the difference between two fractiles.

    a. percentile
    b. interfractile range
    c. quartile
    d. median

_____ 13. The most popular interfractile range is the:

    a. interquartile range
    b. quartile
    c. percentile
    d. percentage

_____ 14. The square of the standard deviation is the _____.

    a. mean deviation
    b. standard deviation squared
    c. variance
    d. quartile

_____ 15. The square root of the variance is the _____.

    a. intervariance
    b. interfractile
    c. mean
    d. standard deviation

_____ 16. Measures of dispersion include:

    a. variance
    b. standard deviation
    c. range
    d. all of the above

_____ 17. Lack of symmetry in a data set is referred to as _____.

    a. peakedness
    b. kurtosis
    c. skewness
    d. curve

_____ 18. Which of the following is not a type of kurtosis?

    a. mesokurtic
    b. endokurtic
    c. leptokurtic
    d. platykurtic

True/False Questions

_____ 1. The mean, the median and the mode are all measures of central tendency.

_____ 2. If there are extreme values in a distribution, the mean is the most accurate measure of central tendency.

_____ 3. If you are studying the number of crimes committed and two criminals have committed 200 crimes in the last 12 months but the second most active criminal committed only 55 crimes, the median would be the appropriate measure of central tendency.

_____ 4. Two samples might have the same mean but have quite different distributions.

_____ 5. To have a complete picture of a set of data, measures of variability such as the standard deviation may be as important as measures of central tendency.

_____ 6. Your pediatrician has just informed you that your child is at the 75th percentile for height for a child her age. This means that 75 percent of the children her age are taller than your child.

_____ 7. Percentile is just another term for percentage.

_____ 8. The standard deviation squared is the variance.

_____ 9. There is only one way to calculate the standard deviation.

_____ 10. The mode is the most frequent score in a distribution.

_____ 11. The median is the 50th percentile.

_____ 12. A mesokurtic curve is a moderately peaked curve.

_____ 13. A lepokurtic curve is a flat curve.

_____ 14. A platykurtic curve is a sharply peaked curve.

_____ 15. Skewness refers to inaccuracy in the distribution.

_____ 16. Only the mean measures how typical a score is.

Essay/Discussion Questions

1. Define/explain the three measures of central tendency. When would you use each? Discuss the advantages and limits of each.

2. Why is variability important to measure? Give some examples of the importance of examining the variability of data sets.

_____
_____
_____
_____
_____
_____
_____
_____
_____
_____
_____
_____
_____
_____
_____
_____
_____
_____
_____
_____
_____
_____
_____
_____
_____
_____
_____
_____
_____
_____
_____
_____
_____

5   The Normal Distribution

KEY TERMS AND NAMES

addition rule
asymptotic
central limit theorem
converse rule
data transformations
distribution of chance
empirical definition
empirical distribution
Gaussian curve
multiplication rule
mutually exclusive

normal curve
probability
random error
raw score
standard score scale
statistical inference
symmetrical about the mean
theoretical definition
unimodal
z distribution
z score

Francis Galton

CHAPTER SUMMARY

I. Introduction

A normal distribution represents the actual distribution of naturally occurring data. If several people were to take measurements of the same item, there would be different measurements, yet a large number of the measurements would cluster around the center of the distribution. Real distributions never completely conform to a strict normal curve, but the larger the population the more it tends to conform to the normal distribution. Inferential statistics take a set of data and "normalize" it so that comparisons can be made.

II. Properties of the Normal Distribution

1. Characteristic bell shape.
2. *Unimodal* (there is only one mode).
3. The mean is located at the point where the curve would balance. If the distribution is perfectly normal, the mean is located at the point where a vertical line can cut the bell curve equally in half. If the distribution is skewed, the mean will be pulled out toward the tails of the curve; thus the distribution will not be considered normal.
4. *Asymptotic* (the tails of the curve never actually touch the horizontal axis).
5. The total area under the curve is 100 percent (that is, all of the observations fall under the normal curve).
6. The 50th percentile (the median) is the same value as the mean.

III. The Standard Deviation and the Normal Distribution

In a normal distribution, there is a direct relationship between the standard deviation and the curve. If a set of data is normally distributed, the same number of observations will always fall within the same standard deviation units from the mean of the distribution:

- 68 percent of the observations lie within +1 to -1 standard deviations from the mean
- 95 percent of the observations lie within +2 to -2 standard deviations from the mean
- 99.8 percent of the observations lie within +3 to -3 standard deviations from the mean

For example, if we have a normally distributed data set where the mean is 43.12 and the standard deviation is 4.3, we could say that 68 percent of the data set would lie between 47.42 and 38.82 on the curve and 99.8 percent of the data would lie between the values 30.22 and 56.02.

IV. Standard Scores and the Normal Distribution

It is not very helpful to know what a score is and not know the standard deviation and mean of the data set because until we know the values of the latter, we cannot make comparisons. If we do know these values, we can say where the score lies in regard to the whole distribution. *Z* scores are used to describe units of standard deviation from the mean. One *z* score equals one standard deviation, two *z* scores equals two standard deviations, and so on. A *z* score has a mean of zero and a standard deviation of one. This score is used as a standardized measure. By calculating *z* scores, we can transform any data set to a scale that has a standard deviation of one and a mean of zero.

A. Converting raw scores to *z* scores:

$$z \ = \ \frac{X - \overline{X}}{\sigma}$$

Where: X = the raw score
$\overline{X}$ = the mean for the reference group
σ = standard deviation for the reference group

For example, suppose we have 36 reported incidents of larceny in a certain county during the Christmas period. The mean number of larceny incidents for holiday periods is 24 and the standard deviation is 7. To standardize the score:

$$z = \frac{36 - 24}{7}$$

$$= 1.71$$

This means that the score lies 1.71 units above the mean.

To make more sense of this we need to look at the normal distribution table (see Appendix B of the textbook). Take your z score (in this case, it is 1.71) and look down the column labeled "z"; go down to 1.7 and then move across to the 0.01 column. The value shown is 0.4564. This means that the area between the mean and z is 0.4564 and the area beyond z is 1 − 0.4564 (which is 0.5436). It is important to note that our table depicts only one side of the distribution, a negative z score is identical to a positive z score because the two sides of the distribution are identical. A negative z score simply means that you are below the mean rather than above it.

The next step in using the normal curve is to determine the percentage falling between two raw scores. For example, on an officer proficiency test there was a mean of 500 and a standard deviation of 100. What percentage of officers would score between 340 and 682?

$$z_1 = \frac{340 - 500}{100} = -1.6$$

$$z_2 = \frac{682 - 500}{100} = 1.82$$

When we look up these values in the normal table, we find that $z_1 = 0.0548$ and $z_2 = 0.9656$. Then we must subtract 0.0548 from 0.9656 because we want to know the value that lies between the two. Therefore, 91.08 percent of the officers will score between 340 and 682.

If the z score is given and the question asks for the score, rearrange the formula so that:

$$\overline{X} + (z \times \sigma) = X$$

V. Other Standard Scores

Other standard scores used include the SAT, which has a mean of 500 and a standard deviation of 100; the GRE, which has a mean of 500 and a standard deviation of 100; the Wechsler IQ test, which has a mean of 100 and a standard deviation of 15; the Stanford-Binet IQ test, which has a mean of 100 and a standard deviation of 16; and T scores, which have a mean of 50 and a standard deviation of 10.

Researchers have noted that often we are too quick to assume that a data set is normally distributed. If a data set is not normally distributed there are procedures called data transformations.

VI. Probability and the Normal Distribution

While the normal distribution is based on what *should* happen, a frequency distribution is based on what actually happens. Using the normal distribution, we can make predictions in determining the chance we have of being right or wrong. Probabilities or "odds" can be expressed as a proportion or a percentage.

The probability of an event A is equal to the number of times event A did occur in the past during a large number of experiments or trials divided by the maximum number of times event A could have occurred during these experiments.

A. *Converse rule of probability:* the probability of an event not occurring, or 1 minus the probability of an event that occurs.

B. *Addition rule*: the probability of obtaining any one of several different outcomes equals the sum of their separate probabilities. This rule assumes that the events are mutually exclusive (i.e., the two events cannot occur simultaneously).

C. *Multiplication rule*: the probability of obtaining a combination of independent outcomes equals the product of their separate probabilities. In other words, what is the probability of obtaining one event and another one as well?

VII. The Binomial Distribution

A binomial probability distribution occurs in situations in which:

1. There is a fixed number of observations (N).
2. All observations are independent (i.e., they are unaffected by other trials).
3. Each observation falls into either success or failure.
4. The probability of success (p) is the same for each observation.
5. A binomial distribution has the parameters n (number of successes) and p (probability of success).

$$P(n) = \frac{N! \, (p^n) \, (q^{N-n})}{n! \, (N-n)!}$$

For example, suppose we have a sample population of 12 police officers and the probability that an officer will be involved in a nonfatal shooting incident is 0.22 and the probability of not being involved in a nonfatal shooting is 0.78. What is the probability of three officers being involved in a nonfatal shooting incident?

$N = 12$! = factorial

$p = 0.22$ A factorial is the product of all the positive integers

$q = 1 - p$ from 1 to n. For example, the factorial of 4 (expressed as "4!") would be 24 because $1 \times 2 \times 3 \times 4 = 24$.

$$P(3) = \frac{12! \, (0.22^3) \, (0.78^9)}{3! \, (12-3)!}$$

$P = .25$

VIII. Finding the Mean and Standard Deviation for Binomial Distributions

The more cases there are in a binomial distribution, the closer the distribution is to resembling a normal distribution. The binomial distribution, however, deals only with discrete data. The mean can be found easily:

$$\overline{X} \text{ (mean)} = Np$$

The formula for standard deviation is:

$$\sigma = \sqrt{Np(1-p)} \quad \text{or} \quad \sigma = \sqrt{Npq} \quad (q = 1 - p)$$

For example, if we have a sample of 300, and $p = 0.22$, the mean is:

$$\overline{X} = 300 \times 0.22$$
$$= 66$$

The standard deviation is:

$$\sigma = \sqrt{Np(1-p)}$$
$$= \sqrt{66 \times (0.78)}$$
$$= \sqrt{51.48}$$
$$= 7.175$$

Because the binomial distribution is similar to the normal distribution, we can use the z score formula instead of the binomial formula. For example if we take the problem of the three officers that may be involved in nonfatal shootings and use the z score formula to solve it, we obtain:

$$z = \frac{X - \overline{X}}{\sigma}$$

First we have to calculate the mean and the standard deviation.

The mean is: 6.6 (30 × 0.22).
The standard deviation is: 2.27 (6.6 × 0.78 = 5.15; square root of 5.15 is 2.27).
Then plug these values into the z score formula:

$$z = \frac{3 - 6.6}{2.27}$$
$$z = -1.59$$

Using the normal distribution with probability: The normal distribution is used with probability when we do not know the value of n, but we know or can calculate the value of the mean, the standard deviation and the fact that the distribution is normally distributed. We then find a z score and use the normal table to find the probability. Suppose the mean score of police department A on the entrance exam is 63, with a standard deviation of 8.2. What is the probability that an officer will score 55 or less?

$$z = \frac{55 - 63}{8.2}$$
$$= -0.97$$

Look at the normal table (see Appendix B of the textbook). You will find the proportion of 0.3340. Therefore, the probability that an officer will score 55 or less is 33.40 percent.

We would use the multiplication and addition rules when there are several probabilities to be found.

IX. Central Limit Theorem

The *central limit theorem* allows researchers to sample an unknown population and compare the sample to a normal distribution in order to make inferences about the unknown population. If a sample is sufficiently large (i.e., 100 or more), then the sampling statistics from that sample (the mean and standard deviation) will be normally distributed.

EXERCISES

Short-Answer Questions

1. With a mean of 7.5 and standard deviation of .75, convert the following raw scores into z scores:

    a.   3.5 = _____

    b.   7.9 = _____

    c.   10.11 = _____

2. Convert a z score of 2.5 with a standard deviation of 1.15 and a mean of 72 to a raw score:_____.

3. What is the probability of:

    a.   drawing the ace of spades from a shuffled deck of 52 cards?_____

    b.   drawing two black cards from two decks of 52 cards?_____

    c.   getting tails on all four flips of a coin?_____

4. What is the probability of a person guessing on a 20-item true/false test and obtaining 15 or more correct?

    a. Solve the problem using the binomial distribution formula.

    b. Solve the problem using the normal (z) distribution.

Multiple-Choice Questions

_____ 1. The theoretical distribution that tends to represent the actual distribution of many actual data sets is known as the:

    a. normal curve
    b. normal distribution
    c. Gaussian curve
    d. all of the above

_____ 2. _____ was a statistician famous for his work on fingerprinting.

    a. Galton
    b. Darwin
    c. Gauss
    d. LaPlace

_____ 3. Real distributions are also called _____.

    a. theoretical distributions
    b. empirical distributions
    c. actual distributions
    d. none of the above

_____ 4. The _____ _____ is used to describe the distribution of normally occurring phenomena.

    a. Galton curve
    b. Galton distribution
    c. normal distribution
    d. population curve

_____ 5. A form of statistics that allows decisions to be made regarding hypotheses is termed:

    a. descriptive statistics
    b. inferential statistics
    c. normal curve
    d. statistical element

_____ 6. The normal distribution is a mathematical function that describes the distribution of:

    a. chance
    b. random errors
    c. both a and b
    d. neither a nor b

_____ 7. The normal distribution is _____.

    a. bimodal
    b. trimodal
    c. multimodal
    d. unimodal

_____ 8. The concept that the tails of the curve never touch the horizontal axis is called:

    a. asymptotic
    b. asymmetrical
    c. asymptyl
    d. asymmetry

_____ 9. There is a(n) _____ relationship between standard deviation and variance.

    a. indirect
    b. direct
    c. nondirect
    d. certain

_____ 10. The total area under the normal curve is:

    a. 25 percent
    b. 68 percent
    c. 95 percent
    d. 100 percent

_____ 11. Which of the following is a standard deviation score?

    a. *t* score
    b. *a* score
    c. *z* score
    d. *m* score

_____ 12. Figure 5.5 in the text (see page 95 of text) depicts how many sides of the distribution?

    a. one
    b. two
    c. both
    d. neither

_____ 13. Which of the following is not a standard score?

    a. SAT
    b. GRE
    c. z score
    d. Rorschach

_____ 14. Mathematical procedures used to bring the data more in line with the normal distributions are called:

    a. normal transformations
    b. data transformations
    c. mathematical transformations
    d. data procedures

_____ 15. The answer to the question "what is the chance" is expressed as a:

    a. percent
    b. proportion
    c. probability
    d. ratio

_____ 16. "One minus the probability of an event occurring" is the:

    a. converse rule
    b. multiplication rule
    c. addition rule
    d. subtraction rule

_____ 17. The addition rule is often referred to as the _____ rule.

    a. "and"
    b. "if"
    c. "maybe"
    d. "or"

_____ 18. The multiplication rule is often referred to as the _____ rule.

    a. "or"
    b. "and"
    c. "if"
    d. "maybe"

_____ 19. That no two outcomes will occur simultaneously means that the outcomes are:

    a. mutually exclusive
    b. exhaustive
    c. addition rule
    d. multiplication rule

True/False Questions

———— 1. The normal distribution is bimodal.

———— 2. The central limit theorem stipulates that the mean of many sample means approximates the population mean.

———— 3. A z score tells you how far a raw score deviates from the mean.

———— 4. Professor Jones teaches two sections of Introduction to Statistics. Student Smith earned an 85 on the midterm in the morning section; student Robinson earned an 85 on the midterm in the afternoon section. You can safely conclude that both students were performing equally well.

———— 5. The addition rule is often referred to as the "and" rule.

———— 6. Professor Jones teaches two sections of Introduction to Statistics. Student Smith earned an 89 on the midterm in the morning section; student Robinson earned an 84 on the midterm in the afternoon section. Their z scores, however, are identical. You can safely conclude that both students were performing equally well.

———— 7. To compare two scores from two different samples, it is more helpful to examine z scores than raw scores.

———— 8. The central limit theorem states that the mean z score is zero (0).

———— 9. If you flip a "fair" (nonlopsided) quarter 100 times, you will always get 50 heads and 50 tails.

———— 10. If you draw 13 cards from a standard poker deck, you will draw at least one heart.

———— 11. Although Judge White and Judge Brown both give out the same average sentence for robbers, a convicted robber may still prefer one judge over the other.

———— 12. If the probability of rain is 1.0, you do *not* need to carry an umbrella.

———— 13. Even if probability never helps you to become a better criminal justice professional, it will help you in blackjack.

Essay/Discussion Questions

1. Flip a quarter 100 times and calculate the probability of how many times you will get heads and how many times you will get tails. After the experiment, tell the actual number of times heads and tails came up and express this in percents and proportions.

2. In your own words, explain what a normal distribution is. Why is it important to understand what a normal distribution is?

6 Sampling

KEY TERMS

cluster sample
convenience sample
inferential statistics
nonprobability sample
population
population parameter
probability sample
purposive sample

quota sample
sample
sampling error
simple random sample
snowball sample
statistic
stratified sample
systematic random sample

CHAPTER SUMMARY

I. Introduction

Sampling has many uses. Political polls, for example, can be remarkably accurate. Because it is impossible to obtain every individual's opinion on political issues, a pollster must select a sample or subset of the population to study. Such samples are used to predict what the population will do The *population* includes all possible subjects that can be studied; the *sample* is a subset of the population. For example, a sample of 1,000 people might be questioned about their voting preferences in an upcoming presidential election. This information then can be generalized to the entire voting population.

A numerical measure that describes a sample is called a *statistic*. A numerical measure describing a population is termed a *parameter*. A sample will never give a perfectly accurate picture of what the population will do. The chance of inaccuracy is referred to as *sampling error*.

A. *Sampling in everyday life*: We often use sampling in nonscientific ways. For example, we may ask our friends which products they use. *Consumer Reports* magazine samples and tests various products in order to make recommendations to readers based on their findings. *Consumer Reports,* however, tests only one sample product, whereas political polls test a sizable number of people. This is because the products the magazine tests are supposed to be identical, so testing any one item should produce the same results as testing any other. On the other hand, with people (as in political polls and social science research) one must take human variability into account. There is no basis for assuming that human beings are identical, so larger sample sizes are required for generalizability.

II. Probability Samples

A probability sample is a sample chosen so that the probability of each item being selected into the sample is known. A probability sample should be representative of the population, providing a true picture of what the population is like.

A. *Simple random sample*: The simple random sample is the most basic probability sample. Each unit has an equal chance of being selected. The subjects are chosen at random, for example, by drawing names out of a hat or using a random number table (see Appendix A of the textbook).

B. *Systematic random sample*: In a systematic random sample, subjects still have an equal chance of being selected, but every nth subject is chosen. For example, every tenth student may be chosen from a list of the 10,000 students at Fictional State University, to form a sample of 1,000 students. With this type of sample, problems may occur if the list of the population is arranged in a pattern. For example, if a researcher decides to choose every 20th cell in a prison and every 20th cell happens to be a corner cell, there may be important differences between corner cells and other cells that would influence the study.

C. *Stratified sample:* A stratified sample is used to sample a population that has subgroups that contain small proportions of the population. For example, if a researcher is interested in surveying food preferences on campus and wants to include vegetarians, he or she should be aware that there may not be many vegetarians in the student body. If the student body is only 5 percent vegetarian, first the researcher would obtain a list of people who report themselves to be vegetarians. Then, he or she would take a simple random sample of that sampling frame so that the number chosen would equal 5 percent of her eventual sample.

It is important to be aware that sampling frames (the lists used to select actual sample members) may not always contain all the subjects in a population. For example, the telephone book does not contain all the members of the community. Some people do not have telephones; others request that their phone numbers remain unlisted. Moreover, phone numbers often are out of date before the phone book is even printed.

D. *Cluster sampling*: Cluster sampling involves taking a sample of clusters from a population and then sampling elements from the clusters. An example of a cluster sample would be selecting 20 police departments in the United States and then selecting 100 officers from each of the 20 departments (clusters). This type of sample is especially useful for field studies. Logistically, it is easier to handle than other types of samples.

E. *Other sampling strategies:* A researcher also can use cluster sampling and stratified sampling combined, or probability-proportionate-to-size sampling, which takes into account clusters that differ in size.

III. Nonprobability Samples

The representativeness of a nonprobability sample is unknown. Nonprobability samples are used in situations where there is no sampling frame available, so not every member of the population has an equal chance of being selected.

A. *Availability/convenience sample*: An availability or convenience sample is a sample chosen because it is available, convenient or accessible to the researcher. A classic example is a teacher surveying his or her class. The main problem is that bias can occur. College student samples, for example, are not representative of the general adult population, but instead represent young people who have chosen to pursue higher education. Another example would be interviewing the first 100 people who pass. Another name for an availability or convenience sample is an *accidental sample*.

B. *Quota sample:* A quota sample is a sample in which the researcher knows a characteristic of the population and seeks to obtain that characteristic in the sample. For example, if a researcher knows that the population is one-half male and one-half female, he or she might seek to obtain that proportion by interviewing the first 50 males and the first 50 females encountered in a mall. Notice that quota sampling resembles stratified sampling, except that quota sampling does <u>not</u> employ a random method of selection and is thus a nonprobability sampling strategy.

C. *Snowball sampling:* A snowball sample is a sampling strategy useful in exploratory studies and in situations where there is no readily available list of the population. In snowball sampling the researcher begins with one or a few persons known to belong to the population of interest, and then asks each subject for the names of other persons belonging to the population. For example, there is probably not a list of gay students or vegetarians at your school. but if you know one or two, they can probably give you the names of others.

EXERCISES

Fill-in-the-Blank Questions

1. If a group of 20 people are surveyed from city X, the group is the _____ and city X is the _____.

2. A numeric measure that describes a sample is called a _____.

3. A parameter describes a _____.

4. Samples are _____ completely accurate of the population. (never/sometimes/always)

5. If each subject has a known chance of being selected, the sample is a _____ sample.

6. The simplest type of probability sample is the _____ _____ sample.

7. Systematic random samples involve choosing every _____ subject.

8. A list of an entire population is called a _____ _____.

Multiple-Choice Questions

_____ 1. What theory is the foundation of sampling?

   a. mathematical theory
   b. sampling theory
   c. probability theory
   d. opportunity theory

_____ 2. A sample is:

   a. any subset of a population
   b. all the cases that could be studied
   c. all the cases that should be studied
   d. all of the above

_____ 3. Any numerical measure that describes a sample characteristic is a:

   a. population parameter
   b. sample
   c. statistic
   d. population number

_____ 4. Any numerical measure of a population is a:

   a. statistic
   b. population number
   c. population parameter
   d. sample

_____ 5. We use sampling in a nonscientific way in our daily lives by:

    a. asking friends if they liked a new movie
    b. asking friends how they will vote
    c. asking friends what consumer products they use
    d. all of the above

_____ 6. Nonprobability samples are chosen:

    a. with knowledge of the probability of selection
    b. without clear knowledge of the probability of selection
    c. randomly
    d. none of the above

_____ 7. Which of the following would be an example of an availability/convenience sample?

    a. A researcher chooses to study students at Notre Dame because she thinks it is a typical university
    b. A researcher has 300 students in an introductory class and uses that class as her sample
    c. A researcher selects every tenth student who is enrolled at his university
    d. A researcher interviews some vegetarians she knows and asks them if they can name additional vegetarians

_____ 8. Which of the following would be an example of a snowball sample?

    a. A researcher chooses to study students at Notre Dame because she thinks it is a typical university
    b. A researcher has 300 students in an introductory class and uses that class as her sample
    c. A researcher selects every tenth student who is enrolled at his university
    d. A researcher interviews some vegetarians she knows and asks them if they can name additional vegetarians

_____ 9. Which of the following would be an example of a purposive sample?

    a. A researcher chooses to study students at Notre Dame because she thinks it is a typical university
    b. A researcher has 300 students in an introductory class and uses that class as her sample
    c. A researcher selects every tenth student who is enrolled at his university
    d. A researcher interviews some vegetarians she knows and asks them if they can name additional vegetarians

_____ 10. Snowball sampling is effective in situations in which there is:

    a. a readily available list of the population
    b. agreement that a particular city is a microcosm of the United States
    c. no readily available list of the population
    d. none of the above

_____ 11. The crucial question in purposive sampling is:

    a. Is the sample large enough?
    b. Will anyone be interested in this sample?
    c. Is the sample really typical?
    d. none of the above

_____ 12. A simple random sample can be chosen by:

    a. using a table of random numbers
    b. selecting every person you walk past
    c. drawing names out of a hat
    d. a and c but not b

True/False Questions

_____ 1. In statistics the term population refers to all of the units that could be studied if one had unlimited time and resources.

_____ 2. A good sample is representative of the population from which it is drawn.

_____ 3. Sampling always involves sampling error.

_____ 4. Probability samples are chosen so that the probability of each item being selected is not known.

_____ 5. Purposive samples allow for the use of inferential statistics.

_____ 6. If the population of interest is one-half male and one-half female and if the researcher interviews 50 men and 50 women in a mall, that would be an example of a quota sample.

_____ 7. A purposive sample is a random sample with a definite aim in mind.

_____ 8. A probability sample is chosen in such a way that there is a known probability of selection for each unit selected.

_____ 9. Stratified sampling is used when it is known that a subgroup makes up a small proportion of the population.

Essay/Discussion Questions

1. Explain the difference between probability sampling and nonprobability sampling. Explain the major types of probability samples and nonprobability samples. Discuss the conditions in which you would choose a particular sampling strategy.

2. Assume that your population of interest is the entire student body at your university. How would you go about selecting a random sample of the entire population? What factors would you need to consider?

3. Assume that you are going to select a purposive sample of three universities for a study of three typical universities in the United States. How might you select three "typical" universities? What factors would influence your decision? Name three specific universities and defend your choices.

4. You have chosen to conduct an exploratory study of burglars. Discuss how snowball sampling could be used in this situation.

Experiments and Quasi-Experiments

KEY TERMS

classical experimental design
control group
evaluation research
experimental group
Hawthorne effect
history
maturation
natural experiment

posttest-only design
quasi-experiment
random assignment
Scared Straight documentary
selection bias
simulated experiments
Solomon four-group design
statistical regression to the mean

CHAPTER SUMMARY

I. A Nonexperiment

The *Scared Straight* documentary was a documentary filmed in a New Jersey prison that showed a group of adolescents (some with histories of delinquency and some without) who went into the prison and spoke with inmates who were "lifers." The inmates spoke of the terrifying everyday experiences of prison life. Six months later, the group of adolescents (with one exception) seemed to have been scared out of delinquent behavior because of the consequences. At first, there were claims that they had found a cure for adolescent delinquency, but the so-called "experiment" was missing some vital experimental design features. For example, there was no control group that did not undergo the "treatment" that could be compared against those who did participate. Second, there was no random assignment of teenagers to groups. Both of these are necessary for a true experiment. Some criminologists offered other explanations for the changed behavior of the previously delinquent adolescents. They include the following possibilities:

A. *History*: History refers to outside events that may have influenced the teenagers, such as a delinquency awareness program in their high school.

B. *Maturation*: Maturation refers to the possibility that some of the adolescents may have matured and changed their views on delinquency. (Maturation is one reason why murderers are not paroled until they have served a good portion of their sentence.)

C. *Selection bias*: Selection bias occurs when correct experimental design is not followed. For example, because there was no control group in the Scared Straight program, there is no way to assess whether the teenagers chosen were especially prone to change their behavior patterns. Random assignment to the experimental or the control group assures that selection bias is not a factor.

D. *Statistical regression to the mean*: Statistical regression to the mean can occur when an adequate experimental design is not used. In the Scared Straight example, the subjects were chosen for their tendency to commit delinquent acts. After they saw what prison life was like, their behavior changed to a more normal level, but the behavior change toward normality may have happened without exposure to inmates. In other words, the experiment may not have influenced the subjects in any way at all. Any set of subjects who are performing at an above-average or below-average level will tend to slip back (regress) toward the normal level of performance (the mean), regardless of any other factors that are introduced. Extraordinarily high or low levels often can be attributed to temporary phenomena, and they are likely to change without exposure to outside factors.

E. *Hawthorne effect*: The Hawthorne effect refers to the notion that subjects may change their behavioral patterns because they are participating in an experiment. During a study conducted at the Western Electric Company in the 1930s, productivity increased even when conditions were made more aversive, so it was postulated that it was the mere fact of being studied, rather than the nature of the treatment applied, that produced the effect

   The Hawthorne effect theory, however, has been contradicted on several occasions. First, Rice concluded that productivity increases at the Western Electric Company were not due to observation of the workers, but rather to experience gained by workers, maturation and a different supervision structure. Second, an observational study of police by Black and Reiss indicated that although observation is likely to influence behavior, eventually people will revert back to their normal behavior patterns so an accurate picture can be obtained.

II. Classical Experimental Design

A. *Key elements of classical experimental design:*

1. random assignment of subjects to an experimental or control group
2. pretesting
3. administration of the experimental treatment (intervention)
4. measurement of results or posttesting (which includes comparing the differences between the experimental and control groups)
5. conclusion (if no differences are observed, the experiment did not work)

III. Other Experimental Designs

A. *Posttest-only design:* Posttest-only experiments do not employ a pretest. This type of design is used most often when there is a possibility that a pretest would influence the subjects in some manner as to make the research questionable.

B. *Solomon four-group design*: The Solomon four-group design has two experimental groups and two control groups. One set undergoes the classical experimental design procedure, while the other follows the posttest-only design. This allows a comparison between the two groups to determine whether the pretest had any additional effects on the subjects, independent of the experimental effect.

C. *Natural experiments:* Natural experiments are naturally occurring situations that can be used as experiments. Sometimes ideal situations for research occur. For example, in California, 107 inmates who were on death row were made eligible for parole when the death penalty was temporarily abolished in that state. Researchers looked at the sample to determine recidivism rates. The majority of the 40 murder convicts who were actually paroled made successful transitions back into regular society, while a few did not succeed and committed other crimes. Natural experiments are useful in criminal justice in particular because experiments on crime are frequently difficult to implement and criminal justice officials may be reluctant to participate because of political or public concerns.

  Another opportunity for research occurred in New York when 1,000 patients were released from hospitals for the criminally insane and transferred to civil hospitals. Researchers studied the group and concluded that these patients were not as dangerous as previously thought.

D. *Simulated experiments*: Simulated experiments are staged. One of the most famous simulated experiments is Zimbardo's mock prison experiment conducted at Stanford University. After Zimbardo hired students to act as prisoners and guards for the study, his research team found some disturbing results: the guards became brutal and could not distinguish their part in the experiment as a role as opposed to reality. Likewise, the prisoners could think only about how they could escape. Due to these factors, Zimbardo felt obliged to abandon the experiment after only six days.

IV. Quasi-Experiments

Usually quasi-experiments lack random assignment of subjects to the experimental and control groups, but otherwise follow classical experimental design. Quasi-experiments use a comparison group rather than a control group. Researchers can compare appropriate groups, but the results are not as convincing as those obtained when random assignment is used. In some situations, though, a quasi-experiment is still adequate. McKenzie and Shaw, for example, conducted a quasi-experiment of boot camp prisoners and compared the social skill rates of prisoners in the camps to prisoners in traditional facilities. The boot camps were found to be more effective.

V. Time-Series Analysis

Time-series analysis is research completed over a long period of time that does not have a specific experimental design. Usually, these studies measure the impact that an intervention has over time. An example of this is the Birmingham sting operation.

VI. Other Experiments in the Criminal Justice Setting

A. *Minneapolis domestic violence research*: Domestic violence research conducted in Minneapolis, and then replicated in Omaha and Charlotte, looked at the most effective means for dealing with domestic violence perpetrators (see Chapter 17 of the text for more details). The experiments obtained conflicting results.

B. *Trends in criminal justice research*: In the 1960s there were numerous delinquency/ treatment or prevention projects. In more recent years, there has been a movement toward evaluating different types of policing. Thus, the current political climate seems more conducive to research on policing than on delinquency.

C. *Evaluation research*: Evaluation research is research that attempts to determine whether a program or strategy is effective, whether it is meeting its objectives. One example is the *Scared Straight*-type program. Several studies of such confrontation programs have been conducted to determine if they reduce recidivism.

EXERCISES

Fill-in-the Blank Questions

1. The Hawthorne effect refers to behavioral _____ that subjects make because they are under observation.

2. Quasi-experiments lack _____ _____ of subjects.

3. According to the 1992 RAND study, intensive probation _____ affect the recidivism rate of offenders.

4. The Scared Straight "experiment" lacked a _____ _____ and _____ _____ of subjects.

5. Subjects who are chosen for an experiment because they are prone to change may cause _____ in the experiment.

6. The posttest-only design eliminates the _____.

7. If a group performs extraordinarily in an experiment, and then is retested and the group performs at a normal level, the second result could be attributed to _____ _____ _____.

8. The Solomon experimental design allows a _____ to be done between two experimental groups.

9. Posttest-only experiments are used when the research subjects could be _____ to the research in such a way to contaminate the research.

10. List the five key elements of a classically designed experiment.

1) _____
_____

2) _____
_____

3) _____
_____

4) _____
_____

5) _____
_____

11. Zimbardo's mock prison experiment research is an example of a _____ experiment.

Multiple-Choice Questions

_____ 1. The Scared Straight program at the Rahway Prison involved:

   a. tours of the prison
   b. confrontational rap sessions with prisoners
   c. prisoner descriptions of the horrors of prison life
   d. all of the above

_____ 2. What was the scientific methodological flaw with the _Scared Straight_ documentary?

   a. lack of random assignment to the treatment or the control group
   b. small sample size
   c. lack of a theoretical perspective
   d. all of the above

_____ 3. In research methodology, _history_ means:

   a. the past experiences of the subjects
   b. the political and economic events taking place in the country at the time of the experiment
   c. any outside event that might cause a change in behavior
   d. b and c but not a

_____ 4. Selection bias means:

   a. choosing subjects for the study who are most unlikely to change
   b. choosing subjects who are most favorable to change
   c. choosing subjects who have prejudicial attitudes
   d. a or b but not c

_____ 5. Statistical regression to the mean is:

   a. a statistical test very similar to Pearson's correlation coefficient
   b. the phenomenon of subjects seeming to improve when actually their behavior is simply returning to a true average rate
   c. subjects experiencing temporary discomfort in a medical experiment
   d. none of the above

_____ 6. Key elements of classical experimental design are:

   a. random assignment of subjects to either an experimental group or a control group
   b. administration of the experimental stimulus (treatment)
   c. measuring the results to see if there is any difference between the experimental group and the control group
   d. all of the above

_____ 7. The Solomon four-group design entails:

   a. one experimental group and one control group; both get a pretest and a posttest
   b. any sample with four sub-groups such as: Whites, African-Americans, Hispanics and Other
   c. two experimental groups and two control groups
   d. none of the above

_____ 8. In the Stanford prison experiment prisoners and guards

    a. were no longer able to differentiate between role playing and reality

    b. experienced dramatic changes in virtually every aspect of their behavior, thinking and emotions

    c. showed no adverse effects

    d. a and b

_____ 9. Quasi-experiments lack:

    a. a comparison group

    b. a control group

    c. an experimental stimulus

    d. none of the above

_____ 10. Evaluation research is research that concerns:

    a. program effectiveness

    b. program costs

    c. recidivism rates

    d. none of the above

True/False Questions

_____ 1. The *Scared Straight* documentary utilized a true experimental design.

_____ 2. Maturation means that research subjects become less responsible with age.

_____ 3. The Hawthorne effect suggests that simply paying attention to research subjects can cause dramatic changes in behavior.

_____ 4. The posttest-only design includes a brief, simple pretest.

_____ 5. One problem with pretests is that they might influence the behavior of the subjects.

_____ 6. Natural experiments occur without planning or intervention by researchers.

_____ 7. Simulated experiments are experiences that researchers stage in order to test hypotheses.

_____ 8. A critical question in simulated experiments is how accurately they reflect a real life situation.

_____ 9. Experimental evaluations in correctional settings have emphasized control more than treatment.

_____ 10. The Scared Straight documentary showed that almost all of the youths who went on the prison tour still committed crimes during the six months after the program.

_____ 11. In terms of experimental designs, "history" refers to the prior personal histories of the research subjects.

_____ 12. Maturation is one reason why parolees whose crime had been homicide tend to have low recidivism rates.

_____ 13. In evaluation research, one of the key ingredients is that the program should have clear and measurable objectives.

Essay/Discussion Questions

1. Assume that you are the Research Director for the state Department of Corrections. The state has just authorized a new boot camp program.

    a. Discuss an ideal evaluation plan using a classical experimental design.

b. Discuss obstacles to an ideal research design and modifications that you would probably have to incorporate into the design.

2. Assume that you are the police chief in a department with 350 officers in a city of approximately 250,000 people. Your department has been using two-officer patrol cars and is now considering the feasibility of using one-officer patrols. You have hired a team of researchers to set up an experiment in one or two areas of the city to evaluate the effectiveness and desirability of one-officer patrol compared to two-officer patrol. Discuss the questions that you would want the research to address. Discuss the problems the research team might have in designing an experimental test of the two types of patrol and how the problems might be resolved. How would you get your officers to cooperate with the research?

3. Assume that you are a college professor and you have been awarded a grant to replicate Zimbardo's Stanford Prison Experiment. Is there any way that you could replicate this famous mock prison study in a manner that is both scientific and ethical? Explain why or why not.

8 Survey Research

KEY TERMS AND NAMES

accuracy
contrived scenario
in-person interview survey
National Crime Victimization Survey
nonresponse
response rate
sample

School Crime Survey
self-administered questionnaire
survey research
telephone survey
telescoping
victimization survey

Peter Letkemann
Ralph Weisheit
Lynn Zimmer

CHAPTER SUMMARY

I. Introduction

Survey research is useful for gathering information such as the number and percent of people who favor capital punishment. It is also useful for testing hypotheses on large samples of respondents.

II. Types of Survey Research

A. *Three basic types of survey research*:

1. Self-administered questionnaires (these can be sent out by mail, distributed in classrooms, etc.)
2. In-person surveys (interviews)
3. Telephone surveys

B. *Advantages of survey research*:

1. Large amounts of data can be gathered on large samples.
2. They can be relatively quick compared to other types of research. (Telephone and mail surveys can be conducted in short time periods)
3. They are relatively inexpensive.

III. Varieties of Survey Research

Several examples of survey research are given in the chapter.

A. Lynn Zimmer's survey of female prison guards is an example of innovative research because the subjects in the study were working in male prisons and because open-ended questions were used, which allowed a wider scope of issues to surface. Although this approach is time consuming, a lot more information can be learned. For example, Zimmer found that the female guards used an inventive role to deal with male prisoners that involved making use of their status as women.

B. Ralph Weisheit conducted in-person interviews with marijuana growers in Illinois. He categorized growers as profit-seekers or people who wanted to maintain a certain lifestyle. He used open-ended interviews to gain an in-depth portrait of the growers.

C. Peter Letkemann conducted an open-ended interview survey with convicted bank robbers and safecrackers in Canada. He took the viewpoint that these criminals treated robbery as their occupation and thus gave us a complete picture of the professional bank robber.

D. *Contrived scenarios* in survey research involve a hypothetical situation. For example, in Rosenbaum and Prinsky's study of mental hospitals in Southern California, different psychiatric facilities were questioned regarding the diagnosis of a hypothetical teenager with hypothetical symptoms. This method allowed the researchers to focus on a precise issue. Another example is La Piere's study in which he accompanied a Chinese couple to 250 hotels and restaurants in the United States to examine the extent of racism. He then sent surveys to the same businesses and found the results were contradictory, thus illustrating a major problem of surveys: the fact that how people act and what they report may not be the same.

IV. Problems with Survey Research

A. *Nonresponse:* One of the major problems of survey research is that some people will fail to respond. Babbie contends that a response rate of 50 percent is adequate, 60 percent is good and 70 percent is very good. This, however, depends largely on the topic of the research and its degree of sensitivity.

B. *Ways to increase the response rate*:

1. Use special strategies for sensitive issues. For example, booklets for written responses were used in the Kinsey Study for questions relating to sexual behaviors.
2. Use monetary or other remuneration;
3. Use postcard reminders
4. Send out a second questionnaire.

C. Survey research accuracy should always be addressed. Self-report surveys especially are not perfectly accurate because people tend to exaggerate or cover up behavior. Teens, for example, may not give accurate accounts of delinquent activity.

D. Paying inmates for participation in research can bias results because the response rate is likely to be very high. This is due to the lack of money-making opportunities in prison. Some topics of a more sensitive nature may obtain more accurate results with nonmonetary rewards.

E. Who conducts interviews is important. A male respondent, for example, may exaggerate his sexual behavior to a female interviewer.

F. Getting to know the subjects helps accuracy.

G. One author makes a distinction between paying a respondent for his or her time rather than his or her responses. This reduces any pressure to make up or fabricate responses.

V. Example of Steps in a Typical Survey Project

A. Topic selection.

B. Literature review. Read about the topic to see if it has been researched previously. This helps establish the strengths and shortcomings of prior research and will help narrow your topic and how you want to research it.

C. Measurement selection. Decide what questions you want to use and how you want to conduct the survey.

D. Sample selection. Decide the sample size and location. Obtain permission from appropriate authorities, if necessary.

E. Questionnaire preparation and processing.

F. Data analysis. Analyze the information gleaned from the questionnaires.

G. Reporting the results.

VI. National Crime Victimization Survey (NCVS)

A. *Victimization statistics:* The National Crime Victimization Survey (NCVS) provides estimates of personal and household victimization rates. In 1991, 24 percent of American homes were touched by crime in some way. Overall, victimization rates were found to be decreasing. Victimization surveys also provide information about offenders. In 1989 the Bureau of Justice Statistics also conducted the School Crime Survey, which researched school crime and such related matters as the availability of drugs and alcohol at schools.

B. *Problems in measuring victimization:*

1. Respondents can forget an event or decline to report it.
2. Respondents can mistakenly place an event in the incorrect time frame (telescoping). (Asking about a specific time period can help this problem.)
3. The technique can overemphasize minor crimes.
4. Respondents are often confused over the legal definition of a crime.

VII. Survey of State Prison Inmates

Conducted by the Bureau of Justice Statistics, the Survey of State Prison Inmates uses face-to-face interviews with inmates to provide information on demographics of inmates and their offense histories.

EXERCISES

Fill-in-the-Blank Questions

1. Three basic types of survey research are telephone surveys, _____ and _____.

2. Two advantages of survey research are _____ and _____.

3. A major problem with survey research is _____.

4. Two problems with victim surveys are _____ and _____.

5. The number of people who answer a survey concerning a _____ topic may be lower than for other types of survey research.

Multiple-Choice Questions

_____ 1. The three types of survey research do *not* include _____.

   a. canvassing
   b. self-administered questionnaires
   c. in-person interviews
   d. telephone surveys

_____ 2. A major advantage of survey research is:

   a. it is time consuming
   b. it is expensive
   c. its ability to gather large amounts of information
   d. it can gather very qualitative, in-depth data

_____ 3. The Bureau of Justice Statistics conducts a survey of citizens every year to measure _____.

   a. fear of crime
   b. attitudes toward crime and the criminal justice system
   c. victimizations
   d. all of the above

_____ 4. _____ did a study of women correctional officers.

   a. Letkemann
   b. Weisheit
   c. Sutherland
   d. Zimmer

_____ 5. _____ did a study of marijuana growers.

   a. Letkemann
   b. Weisheit
   c. Sutherland
   d. Zimmer

_____ 6. _____ did a study of safecrackers.

    a.   Letkemann
    b.   Weisheit
    c.   Sutherland
    d.   Zimmer

_____ 7. Stories that are used to illicit responses are called

    a.   concurred scenarios
    b.   content scenarios
    c.   construct scenarios
    d.   contrived scenarios

_____ 8. According to the text, one of the biggest problems in conducting survey research is

    a.   expense
    b.   nonresponse
    c.   the length of the survey
    d.   the time spent on the survey

_____ 9. Which is *not* a way recommended by the text to increase response rate?

    a.   compensation
    b.   pretest
    c.   reminder postcards
    d.   threats

_____ 10. Another important issue with survey research is

    a.   accuracy
    b.   effort
    c.   time
    d.   monetary costs

_____ 11. The preliminary stage(s) of survey research involve(s): _____.

    a.   definition of the problem
    b.   topic selection
    c.   review of the literature on the topic
    d.   all of the above

_____ 12. After the preliminary stages of survey research, the next step involves _____.

    a.   measurement selection
    b.   summary
    c.   results
    d.   identifying the problem

_____ 13. In 1989 the National Crime Victimization Survey added a special supplement called the

    a.   Youth Crime Survey
    b.   Adolescent Crime Survey
    c.   School Crime Survey
    d.   Teenager Crime Survey

_____ 14. The NCVS provides information on all of the following except:

    a. reported crime
    b. offender characteristics
    c. victim characteristics
    d. dynamics of the victimization experience

_____ 15. Victimization studies such as the NCVS involve such problems as:

    a. memory loss
    b. telescoping
    c. lack of clarity in terminology
    d. all of the above

_____ 16. Which of the following strategies have been used to improve the response rate in surveys?

    a. paying the respondents
    b. using female interviewers
    c. using an ex-offender to interview prisoners
    d. all of the above

_____ 17. Victimization can be

    a. personal or impersonal.
    b. personal or household.
    c. violent or theft.
    d. all of the above.

True/False Questions

_____ 1. Self-administered questionnaires can only be mailed to the subjects.

_____ 2. A large percentage of the women guards in the prisons Zimmer studied adapted by using what Zimmer calls an inventive role; they used their abilities and qualities related to their status as women to deal with the male prisoners.

_____ 3. Weisheit found that all marijuana growers were in business out of a commitment to a lifestyle.

_____ 4. Letkemann studied safecrackers and bank robbers and found that they have occupational problems just like workers in other jobs.

_____ 5. Rosenbaum and Prinsky's study of 12 psychiatric centers provides no support for labeling theory.

_____ 6. In 1934 LaPiere accompanied a Chinese couple throughout the United States stopping at about 250 hotels and restaurants. Only one establishment refused to serve the couple, but a survey of the businesses found that over 90 percent of the responding establishments would not serve the Oriental couple. Thus, the study demonstrated that what people report is not always congruent with how they behave.

_____ 7. One of the biggest difficulties with survey research is the issue of nonresponse. Many people throw questionnaires away or just never return them.

_____ 8. Some authorities agree that an acceptable response rate is about 50 percent.

_____ 9. A survey about a sensitive topic such as date rape may result in a low but acceptable response rate, perhaps as low as 40 percent.

_____ 10. The Kinsey Institute survey on sex and morality in 1980 found that a booklet on sensitive questions was more effective in obtaining responses than in-person interview questions.

_____ 11. In self-report surveys, some adolescents might wish to exaggerate their criminal careers to impress their friends or to boost their own egos.

_____ 12. Gold's study of the self-report technique concluded that 30 percent of the teens he studied were clearly lying.

_____ 13. Cromwell, Olson and Avary's study of drug addicts found that it takes only one or two interviews to get an accurate assessment of such behaviors as illicit drug use.

_____ 14. Faupel feels that paying an offender for information may lead the offender to fabricate information based on the expectation that the researcher wants a certain amount of information.

_____ 15. A recent national School Crime Survey found that about 50 percent of both male and female students reported that they had experienced a victimization at school.

_____ 16. In 1991, 2 percent of American households (almost 23 million) were touched by crime.

_____ 17. Household victimization has remained steady from 1986 to 1991.

_____ 18. Males, persons aged 20-24, blacks, Hispanics, low-income individuals and central-city residents experience the highest victimization rates in their respective demographic groups.

_____ 19. Telescoping refers to the tendency to report victimizations even though they actually occurred prior to the time reference period (e.g., six months) used in the survey.

_____ 20. One criticism of victimization surveys is that they may overemphasize minor crimes.

Essay/Discussion Questions

1. Suppose that in this research methods class, the instructor asks you to develop a topic, select a sample, and construct a questionnaire. Discuss how you would go about overcoming the problems that have been discussed in this chapter.

2. You are contracted with the State Correctional Board to do a survey of the prisoners in that state. You are to find out what the inmates' needs are. Explain which of the basic types of surveys you would use and discuss why you chose that one.

_____

_____

_____

_____

_____

_____

_____

_____

_____

_____

_____

_____

_____

_____

_____

_____

_____

_____

_____

_____

_____

_____

_____

_____

_____

_____

_____

_____

_____

_____

_____

3. Surveys are often considered to be simple opinion polls. Discuss how survey research can be used in innovative ways. Show how survey research can be used to answer more complex research questions.

4. You have been hired to conduct a victimization survey on your college campus. (Assume that there are approximately 5,000 residence hall students and about 5,000 commuting students.) Discuss the problems you foresee conducting a victimization survey of such a college population. How would it differ from the victim surveys the Bureau of Justice Statistics conducts every year? How would it be similar? What solutions would you put in place for problems unique to this population? What solutions would you attempt for problems common to victimization surveys in general?

5. One of the major problems in survey research is the problem of nonresponse. Discuss why nonresponse is a problem. Are there any creative solutions for the problem of nonresponse?

9

Data Collection Issues

KEY TERMS

concurrent validity
construct validity
content analysis
content validity
exhaustive questions
face validity
factor analysis
fixed-response items
format
item analysis
latent content
manifest content

mutually exclusive questions
open-ended items
participant observation
predictive validity
questionnaire
reliability
response-set bias
self-report survey
split-half method
social desirability
test-retest method
validity

CHAPTER SUMMARY

I. Questionnaire Construction

A. *Time and space considerations*: Most people do not want to spend hours participating in surveys. Length depends on the subject matter, but guidelines for maximum time limits have been suggested. Telephone surveys should take no longer than 20 minutes, mailed questionnaires no longer than 30 minutes and in-person interviews no longer than 45 minutes.

B. *Attractive format:* Attractively presented material will help increase the response rate.

C. *Constructing the questionnaire:* Research your topic and see what items have been used in the past. Using items that have been used before can help your study to be valid (accurate) and reliable (consistent).

Devising new items means running the risk of having methodological flaws. A further advantage of borrowing items is that it enables a comparison of results with other studies that have used the same measures.

D. *Fixed-response items vs. open-ended items*: Fixed-response items are items that provide response choices for the respondent, such as agree or disagree. Open-ended items allow the subject to provide any answer. Fixed-response questions make coding and tabulation easy, but may not provide the depth and quality of response that open-ended questions can.

E. *Exhaustive and mutually exclusive questions*: Fixed-response answers should be mutually exclusive (they have only one possible answer) and exhaustive (all the possible answers are included.

F. *Vocabulary level:* Questionnaires should use simple wording in order to avoid ambiguity and bias. The instructions should be straightforward and easy to understand.

G. *Response-set bias:* Response-set bias can affect questionnaires and interview schedules. Response-set bias is present when the questions are worded in such a way as to influence the answers. *Acquiescence response-set bias* refers to the tendency of a set of items to elicit positive responses. *Social desirability response-set bias* means that items are likely to elicit responses that conform with social expectations. Social desirability response-set bias would be evident in a question that asks, "Are you prejudiced against minorities?" Regardless of their true attitudes, most people would not admit to racial or ethnic prejudice.

II. Validity and Reliability

Validity refers to the extent to which an empirical measure adequately reflects the real meaning of the concept under consideration. Validity concerns how accurate the measure is. Reliability means that if we measure the same thing repeatedly, the results will be the same with each measure. If a measure is valid, it will be reliable. However, a study that is reliable may not always be valid. For example, we could measure the length of a table by using a book and counting how many times the book fits on the table. Our results would be the same every time, so it is reliable, but it is not valid because there are more accurate ways of measuring a table, such as using a tape measure.

A. *Validity*

1. *Face validity:* Face validity means that the measure is one that most people agree on and that is logical. For example, most people would agree that you measure a table with a tape measure. Most people would agree that asking a person how satisfied he or she is with his or her job is one valid measure of job satisfaction.

2. *Concurrent validity:* Concurrent validity exists if a measure correlates highly with other measures of the same concept or phenomenon. For example, if a person's score on the SAT is high, we would expect his or her score on the ACT to be high as well, since both tests are supposed to measure an individual's aptitude for college.

3. *Content validity*: Content validity refers to the degree to which a measure covers the range of meanings included within the concept. Whatever large area is valid, then the subgroups within it are also valid. For example, in a valid statistics test, all the subgroups within that test (e.g., the section on chi-square and *t* tests) are also valid. If you are measuring job burnout, the measure of burnout should measure all aspects of job burnout, including emotional exhaustion, depersonalization and lack of personal accomplishment.

4. *Construct validity*: Construct validity compares the validity of one concept or phenomenon to another, but the two must be theoretically related. If no relationship is found, then the theory or measurement was not valid.

5. *Predictive validity:* Predictive validity refers to the ability of a measure to make an accurate prediction. For example, a valid measure of school success potential should correlate with actual school performance.

B. *Reliability*

Reliability refers to the consistency of a measure, including consistency over time. The following are ways to test reliability:

1. *Test-retest method*: The test-retest method means that subjects retaking the same test or participating in the same survey at a later date should record the same results. For example, an individual's IQ score should be similar from a test given in October to the same test administered a few months later.

2. *Split-half method*: The split-half method involves one administration of a test with random halves of the test being intercorrelated. If the results correlate relatively well, internal consistency (reliability) is assumed. In other words, the items of the test are consistent with one another.

3. *Pretesting:* Pretesting the questionnaire is also a good idea. The researcher can use feedback from participants to improve the test before giving it to the actual sample.

IV. Measurement in Other Contexts

A. *Content analysis*: Content analysis is the analysis of existing data from books, paintings, magazines, movies, television shows, etc. *Manifest content* refers to something visible that has an obvious count, such as how many times the word "love" appears on a page of a romance novel. This method is high in reliability but may not necessarily be high in validity. *Latent content* refers to that which is hidden or not immediately obvious, a message or meaning. Latent content analysis is more time consuming and its reliability may be low, but it may be higher in validity.

B. *Participant observation*: Participant observation is research in which the researcher acts as both an observer and a participant. One advantage of participant observation is that the researcher can view subjects in their natural environments so respondents are less disturbed. The method is useful for gathering data on groups about which little is known. Participant observation can be extremely valid: you can ask better questions because in a longer process you can change bad questions and measurements. The disadvantages of participant observations are the researcher's lack of control over the environment, the lack of quantification (only gross counts take place) and often a smaller sample size that makes it difficult to generalize results to the entire population.

A researcher who undertakes this type of research would first keep a log or journal. Then, behavioral notes would be filed under headings (e.g., in a study of excessive force by law enforcement officers, one might use "physical force" and "psychological force"). Modern technological advances, such as laptop computers and hidden video cameras, can augment this type of research.

V. Asking the Right Questions

Regardless of the sophistication level of the researcher's methodology, if the correct questions are not addressed, the value of the results will be questionable. It is crucial that a researcher decide what questions and issues need to be addressed.

EXERCISES

Fill-in-the-Blank Questions

1. If a measure is valid, it will always be _____.

2. A study has _____ if the measures in the study are accurate.

3. If an answer choice provides all the possible answers, then the question is _____.

4. To ask if the respondent is male or female is an example of a question that is _____ _____ .

5. The text recommends that telephone surveys be limited to about _____ minutes.

6. This type of validity exists if a measure correlates well with other measures of the same concept: _____ _____ .

7. One way of testing reliability is: _____.

8. If the results of a study can be used to predict some sort of outcome, the study has _____ _____ .

Multiple-Choice Questions

_____ 1. According to the text, ideally, phone surveys should take approximately ____ minutes.

   a. 15
   b. 30
   c. 50
   d. 80

_____ 2. A questionnaire should look:

   a. cluttered
   b. confusing
   c. attractive
   d. colorful

_____ 3. Which is *not* a reason cited in the text for using previously designed questions?

   a. accuracy
   b. time savings
   c. a history of problems with specific questions
   d. low cost

_____ 4. Questions that are subjective in nature are called ____ items.

   a. probing
   b. fixed-response
   c. open-ended
   d. closed-ended

_____ 5. Questions that are objective in nature are called _____ items.

    a. probing
    b. fixed-response
    c. open-ended
    d. essay

_____ 6. Exhaustive questions are:

    a. fill-in-the-blank
    b. ambiguous
    c. ones that include all possible response choices
    d. multiple-choice

_____ 7. Mutually exclusive questions:

    a. overlap
    b. do not overlap
    c. could overlap
    d. are nonspecific

_____ 8. Survey questions do *not* measure:

    a. attitudes
    b. opinions
    c. behavior
    d. intelligence

_____ 9. Response-set bias is a problem that affects the _____ of survey research.

    a. validity
    b. reliability
    c. predictive validity
    d. response rate

_____ 10. Validity refers to the _____ of a measure.

    a. honesty
    b. accuracy
    c. reliability
    d. consistency

_____ 11. A source of invalidity may be:

    a. brief questions
    b. legal questions
    c. lack of clarity in questions
    d. long questions

_____ 12. If items appear to be clear and logical questions about the topic at hand, they are said to have:

    a. predictive validity
    b. content validity
    c. concurrent validity
    d. face validity

_____ 13. The extent to which a measure appears to conform to prediction is referred to as:

    a. predictive validity
    b. construct validity
    c. content validity
    d. concurrent validity

_____ 14. Which of the following is a frequent criticism of intelligence testing?

    a. it does not correlate well with school performance
    b. it measures middle-class background
    c. it measures a person's criminality
    d. it measures a person's pathological tendencies

_____ 15. Reliability refers to _____ in measurement.

    a. validity
    b. accuracy
    c. consistency
    d. lack of error

_____ 16. If one half of the questions on the Scholastic Aptitude Test (SAT) correlate highly with the other half, that is an example of passing the:

    a. test-retest
    b. validity test
    c. physical test
    d. split-half test

_____ 17. The technique that determines which items correlate most highly with each other and thereby reflect an underlying dimension is called:

    a. burnout
    b. chi-square
    c. standard deviation
    d. factor analysis

_____ 18. One way to improve a questionnaire would be to do a:

    a. pretest
    b. preliminary test
    c. posttest
    d. comparison test

_____ 19. The study of various forms of communication, such as television shows, movies, newspaper articles, books or magazines, is called:

    a. factor analysis
    b. content validity
    c. content analysis
    d. construct validity

———— 20. In content analysis obvious or straightforward interpretations of the material being studied are referred to as:

    a. latent content analysis
    b. manifest content analysis
    c. underlying content analysis
    d. subtlety content analysis

———— 21. Humphreys's study of tearooms (public restrooms) is an example of which type of data collection strategy?

    a. factor analysis
    b. survey
    c. participant observation
    d. experiment

———— 22. ————— can be effective instruments when conducting participant observation.

    a. video cameras
    b. tape recorders
    c. laptop computers
    d. all of the above

———— 23. Fundamental building blocks for collecting potentially useful data include:

    a. asking the right questions
    b. collecting the right data
    c. both a and b
    d. neither a nor b

True/False Questions

———— 1. According to the text, concerning maximum time limits, telephone surveys should take no longer than 20 minutes, mailed questionnaires no longer than 30 minutes and in-person interviews no longer than 45 minutes or an hour.

———— 2. According to the text, concerning ideal time limits, it should take no longer than 10 to 15 minutes to complete telephone surveys, 15 minutes for mail surveys, and less than 30 minutes for in-person interview surveys.

———— 3. Format refers to such matters as making the questionnaire easy to read and keeping it uncluttered.

———— 4. Previously devised measures are always entirely problem-free regarding their validity and reliability.

———— 5. An example of an open-ended item would be a question that asks if a person favors capital punishment and the only two response choices are "agree" or "disagree."

———— 6. An example of an open-ended question would be "Are you satisfied with your job? Explain."

———— 7. Objective test questions and fixed-response survey questions usually require more work up front than essay test questions or open-ended survey items.

_____ 8. Essay test questions and open-ended survey questions are usually easier to devise but harder to score than objective questions and fixed-response survey items.

_____ 9. Miller advises keeping open-ended questions to a minimum and placing them at the beginning of the questionnaire to ensure that the fixed-response items will be answered.

_____ 10. A fixed-response survey questionnaire item measuring income that had no place for persons earning more than $100,000 would be deficient because it was *not* exhaustive.

_____ 11. A question to which a respondent can answer agree or disagree is called a double-barreled question.

_____ 12. The fact that most individuals would say that they abhor racial prejudice is an example of acquiescence response-set bias.

_____ 13. The fact that most individuals say they are satisfied with their jobs is an example of social desirability response set-bias.

_____ 14. A simple way to guard against acquiescence response-set bias is to reverse the wording of some items to make them negative.

_____ 15. Reliability refers to the accuracy of a measure.

_____ 16. To measure job burnout, one instrument includes the statement, "I feel burned out." Such an item is an example of a measure that has face validity.

_____ 17. If two measures of job satisfaction on the same sample of correctional officers correlate highly, that is an example of concurrent validity.

_____ 18. Many argue that the Uniform Crime Reports are lacking in content validity because they do not have enough measurement of white-collar crime.

_____ 19. If only street crime is considered, the Uniform Crime Reports are a good measure of street crime because they include counts of different domains or types of street crime: murder, robbery, rape, burglary, aggravated assault, larceny and auto theft.

_____ 20. A measure has predictive validity if it can be used to make accurate predictions of future performance.

_____ 21. Validity refers to consistency in measurement.

_____ 22. Travis Hirschi's measure of delinquency has been criticized for triviality: many of the items can apply to actions that may be delinquent but are not all that serious.

_____ 23. Content analysis is the study of various forms of communications, including books, magazines, newspapers, songs, paintings, movies, speeches, letters, laws and constitutions.

_____ 24. Manifest content analysis would involve an overall assessment of a topic; it is a more subjective judgment of the content of the material under study.

_____ 25. Manifest content analysis refers to rather obvious matters such as simple counts.

_____ 26. Pretesting is exactly what the term implies: giving a preliminary version of a questionnaire to a small number of respondents so that potential problems with the instrument can be discovered prior to general administration of the questionnaire.

_____ 27. According to Fine, observers do not observe everything and they do not observe perfectly.

Essay/Discussion Questions

1. The personnel manager for the state Department of Corrections has asked you to survey her employees about their job satisfaction. Construct five questions that probe job satisfaction and important related matters. (Do *not* ask such basic demographic questions as age, sex, race.)

1) _____

2) _____

3) _____

4) _____

5) _____

2. You have decided to conduct an in-person interview study of police stress in a department of approximately 200 police officers. Discuss question-wording issues in such a study. What question-construction issues would you face and how would you handle them?

3.   You have been awarded a grant to conduct a study of prison life. You are going to study 100 prisoners at a state prison. Discuss question-wording issues in such a study and possible ways to make the study measures as valid and accurate as possible.

4. Discuss possible content analysis studies of current television shows relating to crime and criminal justice. What topics might be interesting to study? What might you want to study about such shows?

10

Other Research Methods

KEY TERMS

cohort studies
crime clock
ethnocentrism
going native
hidden recordings
Klockars's study: *The Professional Fence*
life histories
longitudinal research designs
Marquart's prison research
meta-analysis
nonlongitudinal studies

objectivity
panel studies
participant observation
secondary data analysis
staged activity analysis
time dimension
trace analysis
trend studies
Uniform Crime Reports
unobtrusive measures

CHAPTER SUMMARY

I. Participant Observation

In participant observation research, the researcher may get involved with the subjects to varying extents. First, involvement can be in the capacity of a complete observer, where the researcher observes the subjects from a distance and the subjects may or may not know if they are being studied. An example of this type of study would be observing pedestrians to see if they jaywalk. Second, the researcher can be a complete participant, where the researcher hides his or her true identity and enters the group as one of them. An example of this is Humphreys's tearoom study, in which Humphreys deliberately hid his identity and became a "watch queen" to gain the information he needed.

Another example of participant observation research is Goffman's study of mental hospital patients. Goffman became an assistant to the athletic director of the hospital and conducted his research there. Only a few top administrators of the hospital knew about Goffman's research.

II. Problems with Participant Observation Research

A. *Observation of illegal or immoral behavior:* The researcher must consider how the most good will be achieved. In observing illegal behavior, one must determine whether it is better to keep quiet so that one's research can be continued or whether the illegal or immoral behavior should be reported, thereby putting an end to the research.

B. *Staged activity analysis:* Staged activity analysis is ideal for observing illegal activities. With this method, the activity is reconstructed and simulated. For example, burglary plans may be staged so that researchers can observe them even when no illegal activity has actually been committed.

C. *Maintaining objectivity:* It is important to maintain objectivity in participant observation research. When someone does not maintain the proper objectivity, one is said to "go native." This means that the researcher has become too involved with the subject or the topic of research; such involvement affects objectivity. Opposite to this is the notion of ethnocentrism. Ethnocentrism occurs when a person assumes that one's own culture is correct and proceeds to judge all other cultures by one's own standards. Keeping close contacts with advisors and faculty is offered as one possible solution to the temptation of "going native."

III. Life Histories

The use of life histories is a variation of qualitative research in which the researcher constructs the life history of the subject. For example, Faupel studied the lives of 30 heroin addicts and found that addicts view their addiction as a career. Faupel divided the careers into four distinct stages: (1) the occasional user, (2) the stable addict, (3) the freewheeling addict, and (4) the street junkie.

Another example of the life history study is Carl Klokars's study of a professional fence. Klokars studied the life history of one professional fence and sought out the rationales for his behavior.

IV. Unobtrusive Measures

Unobtrusive measures are nonreactive methods of gathering data. The subjects are usually not aware that they are being studied.

A. *Trace analysis*: Trace analysis is the study of deposits, accretion of matter and other indirect substances produced by previous human interaction. Attempts are made to reconstruct, after the fact, the substance of the phenomena.

B. *Hidden recordings*: Hidden video or audio recordings can be used. The advantage of this is subjects will not show any reactivity as long as they do not know they are being taped.

C. *Archival records*: Memoirs, diaries and historical documents contain a great deal of information that can provide a historical overview of criminological issues. Content analysis is the systematic classification and study of the content of media. Secondary analysis entails the reanalysis of data that were previously gathered for other purposes.

V. Longitudinal Research

Longitudinal studies are conducted over a long period of time. In such studies, the researcher can get to know the subjects and has a chance to change inappropriate or incorrect questions and measurements . as the study progresses. The time dimension helps to clarify or solve a question of research.

A. *Trend studies*: Trend studies compare two or more different samples of subjects at two or more points in time.

B. *Cohort studies*: Cohort studies use samples of individuals who were born at about the same time period, and follows them over a period of time.

C. *Rochester Youth Development Study*: The purpose of the Rochester Youth Development Study was to "examine the development of delinquent behavior and drug use in a predominantly high-risk, urban sample." The study found that delinquency reduces attachment to parents and also reduces a youth's commitment to school.

D. *Delinquency in a Birth Cohort: Delinquency in a Birth Cohort* was a book written about a study done of 10,000 males born in 1945 who lived in Philadelphia during their teens. One-third of these youths had contact with the police at least once during this time. It was found that a very small number of these youths were responsible for a great number of crimes. By introducing a time dimension, researchers indicated a need for the juvenile system to pay special attention to repeat offenders.

E. *Time-series analysis*: Time-series analysis can be considered longitudinal research. Time-series analysis examines events over time to see if a program has any impact on the subsequent course of events.

VI. Cross-Sectional Research

A great deal of research is cross-sectional, meaning that it examines phenomena at one point in time. This can enable the researcher to obtain some indication of how social processes develop over time by logical inference and analysis.

VII. Secondary Data Analysis (the Uniform Crime Reports)

The most widely used example of secondary data analysis is the Uniform Crime Reports (UCR), which are official statistics on crime collected by police departments across the United States and compiled and published by the FBI. These statistics are used to estimate crime rates and how police deal with crime. The crime reports are divided into index crimes (serious offenses such as murder, rape, robbery, aggravated assault, burglary, larceny-theft, motor vehicle theft, and arson) and nonindex crimes (the less serious offenses).

A. *Criticisms and problems with the UCR:* There are criticisms of the UCR. First, the UCR includes only crimes that are brought to the attention of the police. This means that many crimes actually committed are not included in the statistics. Victims may be reluctant to report crimes for various reasons: they may fear reprisals from the perpetrator or they may be unsure as to whether their experience actually constitutes a crime. Recording errors are another possible flaw in these statistics.

Reiman has criticized the UCR on the premise that most white-collar crimes do not fit into a category of the UCR. He says that while the UCR reports only street crimes, some white-collar crimes are potentially more harmful to the public. For example, if a company knowingly continues to sell vehicles with gas tanks too close to the back of the car (making the cars likely to explode on impact), it is potentially at fault for many unnecessary deaths.

B. *Steffensmeier and Steifel's analysis of female criminality*: Steffensmeier and Steifel used the UCR to examine the criminal behavior of women as compared to men. They concluded that women are still quite distinct from men in their criminal behavior and that the crimes that have shown the greatest increase for women are larceny, forgery and fraud. The researchers attribute this to several causes: women's traditional role of consumer increases the opportunities for females to commit fraud and larceny (shoplifting) and technological advances in law enforcement have enabled police to enforce the law more effectively in these areas.

C. *Meta-analysis*: Meta-analysis is a type of secondary data analysis that synthesizes results from several research studies on the same topic and then produces a common statistic that summarizes the results of each study.

EXERCISES

Fill-in-the-Blank Questions

1. _____ _____ involves observing subjects and interacting with them.

2. In participant observation the researcher can assume such roles as _____ _____ or _____ _____.

3. A good example of _____ _____ _____ is research that is based on the Uniform Crime Reports.

4. Panel studies and cohort studies are examples of _____ research.

5. The opposite of longitudinal research is _____ research.

6. The technique that attempts to analyze more than one study using statistics is called _____.

Multiple-Choice Questions

_____ 1. In participant observation the researcher can:

    a. function as a complete observer only
    b. function as a complete participant only
    c. use some combination of participating in social life and observing social life
    d. none of the above

_____ 2. An example of staged activity analysis would be:

    a. Marquart's prison research
    b. Cromwell et. al. paying burglars to reconstruct their past burglaries, without actually having them commit a crime, so that the researchers can observe them
    c. Faupel's technique with hard-core heroin users
    d. none of the above

_____ 3. According to the text, the *main* problem(s) in participant observation is/are:

    a. maintaining one's objectivity
    b. being "found out" by the persons you are studying
    c. the cost of implementation is too high
    d. all of the above are correct

_____ 4. The opposite of "going native" is:

    a. imperfect observation
    b. subjectivity
    c. ethnocentrism
    d. objectivity

_____ 5. A person who believes that his or her own perspective is correct and all other perspectives must be judged by that perspective is a/an:

    a. ethnocentrist
    b. pessimist
    c. optimist
    d. none of the above are correct

_____ 6. In life history research the researcher:

    a. refrains from revealing his or her research role
    b. attempts to pass as just another participant
    c. tries to reconstruct the career or life history of the subject
    d. acts as a biographer of the subject(s)

_____ 7. Faupel's phases of a heroin addict's career include:

    a. occasional user
    b. the stable addict
    c. the freewheeling addict
    d. the street junkie
    e. all of the above

_____ 8. One type of unobtrusive measure is:

    a. staged activity analysis
    b. trace analysis
    c. life histories
    d. regression to the mean

_____ 9. Trend studies:

    a. compare two or more different samples of subjects at two or more points in time
    b. study samples of persons born in a certain period over time
    c. use some combination of participating in social life and observing social life
    d. none of the above

_____ 10. An example of secondary data analysis is:

    a. life histories
    b. Marquart's prison research
    c. Humphreys's "tearoom" study
    d. Uniform Crime Reports

True/False Questions

_____ 1. "Going native" refers to getting so immersed in one's study that one begins to take on the perspective of the persons being studied.

_____ 2. The converse of "going native" is ethnocentrism.

_____ 3. "Going native" assumes that one's own culture is correct and judges all other cultures by that standard.

_____ 4. Imperfect observation happens during participant observation when the researcher does not observe and record everything accurately.

_____ 5. Life history techniques have to do with the researcher functioning as a complete observer.

_____ 6. Trace analysis is one type of unobtrusive measure.

_____ 7. Hidden recordings such as tape recorders or videotape recorders are obtrusive measures.

_____ 8. Longitudinal research is research with a time dimension.

_____ 9. Participant observation research includes panel studies, trend studies and cohort studies.

_____ 10. A cohort study usually studies samples of persons born in a certain period over time.

Essay/Discussion Questions

1. If you were going to conduct a participant observation study of a prison, what problems might you encounter? Do you think that there would be a significant danger of over-identifying with the prisoners? What steps would you take to avoid or minimize the problems that might arise in such a study?

2. If you were to conduct a participant observation study of a police department, what sorts of research difficulties might arise? How would you attempt to minimize or avoid any such problems?

3. What is the life history of a college student? What phases does a typical college student pass through on the road to earning a bachelor's degree?

4. How important is longitudinal research? Is it necessary to trace phenomena over time or can cross-sectional studies plus imagination and logical analysis compensate for the lack of a time dimension in a research design? For example, do you think that a study of college life would require a longitudinal dimension or could the right questioning in a cross-sectional study allow you to obtain an adequate picture of college life? Explain.

11

Fundamental Data Analysis: The z Tests

KEY TERMS

alpha level
association hypotheses
confidence intervals
critical region
hypothesis testing
inferential statistics
level of error
level of significance
margin of error
matched-samples z test for proportions
nondirectional hypotheses
nondirectional test
nonparametric
one-sample directional test

one-sample z test
one-tailed test
p value
pooled estimate of the standard deviation
relationship hypotheses
sampling distribution of means
sample size
sampling error
standard error of the difference in proportions
standard error of the mean
two-sample z test
two-tailed test
z test for proportions

CHAPTER SUMMARY

I. Introduction

The normal distribution allows researchers to take a sample of a larger unknown population and compare that sample to the normal distribution. The sample from the larger, unknown population must be sufficiently large and must be randomly selected in order to compare it to the normal distribution. The results from this comparison can then be applied to the real unknown population. This is called *inferential statistics*.

II. Sampling Error

When a researcher infers from samples to populations there will always be some error involved. We can estimate this error and then determine how much confidence can be placed in the outcome of the research. The sampling error can be calculated by subtracting the sample mean from the population mean. Chapter 5 covered the translation of raw scores into z scores to obtain probabilities. Calculating a standard deviation from an unknown population is called finding the standard error of the mean (SE). It is obtained by dividing the sample standard deviation by the square root of the sample size.

$$SE = \frac{\sigma}{\sqrt{N}}$$

By using this formula, we can find a range of mean values on the normal distribution within which the true population mean is likely to fall. We can estimate the probability that our sample mean actually falls within that range of mean values. This is termed a *confidence interval*.

Suppose a state trooper lieutenant wants to estimate the mean number of speeding tickets written per year by his 180 officers. Instead of examining each individual officer, he randomly selects 50 officers and finds that the mean number of tickets they write is 613. The standard deviation is 13. With the normal distribution, we know that 68.26 percent of all random sample means will fall between +1 and –1 standard deviations of the true population mean. To calculate the SE:

$$SE = 13 / \sqrt{50} = 13 / 7 = 1.86$$

Thus the SE of the mean is 1.86.

This must be added to or subtracted from the mean of 618 to determine the range between +1 and –1 standard deviations. Thus, there is a 68.26 percent chance that the mean number of tickets written each year will fall between 619.86 and 616.14. The rule of thumb in statistics is to use the 95 percent confidence interval or better in order for findings to be significant. The 95 percent confidence interval represents between +1.96 and –1.96 standard deviations from the mean, and the 99 percent confidence interval represents +2.58 and –2.58 standard deviations from the mean. If we wanted to be 95 percent confident of the true mean of tickets written per year, we would calculate:

$$614 +/- (1.96 \times 1.86)$$
$$= 613 +/- 3.64$$
$$= 609.36 \text{ to } 616.64$$

As the level of confidence increases, the range also increases.

III. Confidence Intervals and Sample Size

By using the confidence interval, we can determine how big our sample size must be. This is done by calculating a margin of error, usually of +/– 3 percent or +/– 5 percent . The margin of error is dependent upon the population size (N), the sample size (n) and the confidence interval. For example, suppose you were surveying a group of officers in a large department on their opinions of moonlighting. If there were 1,200 officers in the department, how many should you have in your sample?

$$n = (p) (1 - p) [(z / ME)]^2$$

Where: n = sample size
p = population proportion (because we do not know what proportion of police officers will oppose or favor moonlighting, we would use 50 percent or 0.5)

Now plug in the data to the formula:

$$n = (0.5) (1 - 0.5) [1.96/0.5]^2$$
$$= 0.25 (39.2)^2$$
$$= 384.16$$

Therefore, a sample of 384 officers is appropriate for this study. For smaller populations, a second formula can be used to avoid over sampling:

$$n^* = n/ [1+ (n/N)]$$

Where: n^* = the new sample size
$\quad\quad\quad\quad n$ = the sample size determined by the first formula
$\quad\quad\quad\quad N$ = population size

As the population size increases, the required sample size decreases due to the central limit theorem.

There is also a level of error also known as the *level of significance* or *alpha level*. If a researcher has a 95 percent chance of being right in his or her conclusions, there is a 5 percent chance of being wrong.

IV. Hypothesis Testing

The decision to reject the null hypothesis of no difference or to adopt the research hypothesis of difference is based on our significance level or level or error. Thus, a hypothesis must be stated in such a way so it can be statistically tested.

Null hypotheses, as you may recall from chapter 2, are statements of no relationship. This means that when two or more samples are taken from the same population, there is no difference between the samples. Any observed difference is due to sampling error. If the observed differences are large enough to indicate that the difference was not a result of sampling error, then we would reject the null hypothesis in favor of the research hypothesis. Symbolically, we refer to the null hypothesis as H_o and the research hypothesis as H_a.

A.   Types of hypotheses:

1.   *Directional hypotheses:* Directional hypotheses indicate a direction of less or more, or an increase or decrease between the two samples. Whatever the research hypothesis states, the null hypothesis would state the opposite. For example, if the research hypothesis states that there are fewer convicted female murderers on death row than males, then the null hypothesis would state that there are the same number or more female murderers on death row. A directional test is one-tailed because only one side of the normal distribution is considered.

2.   *Nondirectional hypotheses:* A nondirectional hypothesis simply states that there *is* a difference between two or more samples. These are two tailed tests because both sides of the normal distribution are considered.

3.   *Association or relationship hypotheses:* Association or relationship hypotheses consider whether two or more samples are related in some way. For example, we may consider that the more time a person spends exercising, the lower his or her body fat percentage. Thus, the research hypothesis would be that the two variables are correlated or associated, that as one variable increases, the other decreases. The null hypothesis would state that the variables are not associate. Often association or relationship hypotheses have no parameters for comparison, that is, their standard deviations and

means cannot be calculated. An example of this is the relationship between sex (nominal data) and favorite colors (also nominal data). These type of hypotheses require nonparametric statistics, which will be discussed later in the text.

V. Setting the Level of Error

Once we have workable null and research hypotheses, we can decide what level of error we will use. The general rule of thumb is to use 95 percent confidence (or 0.05 level or error) but this will depend on the type of study being undertaken.

Statistical errors are known as Type 1 or Type 2 errors. Type 1 errors are instances in which a true null hypothesis is rejected. Type 2 error occurs when a truly false null hypothesis is not rejected.

VI. The p Value

The p value (also referred to as the *alpha value*) is used to determine the probability of getting the data we have, given that the null hypothesis is true. A p value of 0.05 means that the null hypothesis is true five times out of every 100. In order to reject the null hypothesis, the p value must be 0.05 or less. If the researcher sets the level of error at 0.05 and the p value is less than 0.05, then the researcher can reject the null hypothesis because this is significant.

VII. One-Sample z Test

The one-sample z test is used when a one-sample mean is being compared to some standard or population mean.

Steps:

1. State H_o and H_a hypotheses.
2. Compute the mean and standard deviation for the sample:

$$\overline{X} = \frac{\Sigma fX}{N}$$

$$\sigma = \sqrt{\frac{\Sigma f(X^2)}{N} - \overline{X}^2} \quad \text{(for a population)}$$

$$s = \sqrt{\frac{\Sigma f(X^2)}{N-1} - \overline{X}^2} \quad \text{(for a sample)}$$

3. Compute the standard error of the mean:

$$SE = \frac{\overline{X}}{\sqrt{N-1}}$$

4. Compute the *z* statistic:

$$z = \frac{\overline{X} - \mu}{SE}$$

      Where: $\overline{X}$ = mean
                 μ = standard mean for comparison
              SE = standard error of the mean

5. Consult a normal (*z*) distribution table to determine area beyond *z* (see Appendix B of the textbook).

6. If the obtained *z* statistic falls beyond the tabled *z* score for the .05 level of error (1.96 for a two-tailed test and 1.65 for a one-tailed test), reject H_o and accept H_a. If it does not, fail to reject H_o (not significant).

VIII. Independent Two-Sample *z* Test

The independent two-sample *z* test is used when two sample means are being compared with each other.

    Steps:

1. State the H_o and H_a hypotheses.
2. Compute the mean and variance for each sample.
3. Compute the pooled estimate of the standard deviation:

$$\sigma_p = \sqrt{(N_1 \times \sigma_1{}^2) + (N_2 \times \sigma_2{}^2) / (N_1 + N_2)}$$

4. Compute the standard error of the mean:

$$SE = \sigma_p \times \sqrt{1\,(N_1 - 1) + 1 / (N_2 - 1)}$$

5. Calculate the *z* statistic:

$$z = \frac{\mu_1 - \mu_2}{SE}$$

6. Consult a normal (*z*) distribution table to determine area beyond *z* (see Appendix B of the textbook).

7. If the obtained *z* statistic falls beyond the tabled *z* score for the .05 level of error (1.96 for a two-tailed test and 1.65 for a one-tailed test), reject the null hypothesis and accept the research hypothesis (significant). If it does not, fail to reject H_o (not significant).

IX. Matched-Samples *z* Test

The matched-samples *z* test is used when one sample is measured twice. Commonly used in before-after research designs.

Steps:

1. State the hypotheses (H_o and H_a).
2. Compute the means for both measures in time.
3. Subtract time 2 from time 1 measure (change) and square. Sum the change squares.
4. Compute the standard deviation of the change scores:

$$\sigma_c = \sqrt{(\Sigma C^2 / N) - (\overline{X}_1 - \overline{X}_2)^2}$$

5. Compute the standard error of mean difference:

$$SE_c = \frac{\sigma_c}{\sqrt{N-1}}$$

6. Compute the z statistic by:

$$z = \frac{\overline{X}_1 - \overline{X}_2}{SE_c}$$

7. Consult a normal (z) distribution table (see Appendix B of the textbook) to determine the area beyond z in the same manner as with the independent two-sample z test.

X. z Test for Proportions

The z test for proportions is used as a test of the hypothesis that two proportions are equal. This is a two-tailed (nondirectional) tests that uses proportions rather than means and standard deviations. They are calculated using 2 x 2 contingency tables (crosstabulations).

A. *Independent Two-Sample z Test for Proportions.*

The formula is:

$$z = p_1 - p_2 / sp_1 - p_2 \quad \text{Where:} \quad p_1 \text{ and } p_2 = \text{sample proportions for group 1 and group 2}$$
$$sp_1 - p_2 = \text{standard error of the difference in proportions}$$

B. *Matched-Samples z Test for Proportions*

The matched-samples z test for proportions is useful for examining two phenomena or characteristics with a single group or sample. The test is commonly applied to opinion responses on two items on a questionnaire (e.g., if a person agreed with one statement and disagreed with another statement on an opinion questionnaire).

The formula is:

$$z = \sqrt{(a - d)^2 / a + d} \quad \text{Where:} \quad a = \text{observations in cell a (upper left corner of the contingency table).}$$
$$d = \text{observatons in cell d (lower right corner of the contingency table).}$$

C. Comparing the obtained z statistic for proportions to the normal (z) distribution table is accomplished in the same manner as the other z tests.

EXERCISES

Short-Answer Questions

1. Conduct a one-sample z test with the following data using a standard mean of 70 for comparison. Use a two-tailed test of significance at the .05 level of error.

    $$\underline{X}$$
    100
    90
    80
    70
    60

    State a conclusion:

2. Conduct an independent two-sample z test for the following data. Test the hypothesis: H_o: $\mu_1 = \mu_2$ at the .01 level of error.

$\underline{X_1}$	$\underline{X_2}$
5	8
6	7
4	9
5	8
7	8

    State a conclusion:

3. Conduct a matched-samples z test for the following data. Test the hypothesis: H_o: $\mu_1 = \mu_2$ at the .05 level of error.

Before	After
50	45
40	60
50	55
30	45
20	40

State a conclusion:

Multiple-Choice Questions

_____ 1. Inferences made from samples to populations will always be subject to:

   a. sampling error
   b. operationalization
   c. both a and b are correct
   d. none of the above

_____ 2. Statistical inference:

   a. is an acceptable level of error in survey research
   b. is the decision to reject or fail to reject the null hypothesis
   c. uses the mathematics of probability to provide a way for estimating sampling error
   d. none of the above

_____ 3. The confidence interval "rule of thumb" is to use what confidence interval(s)?

   a. 68 percent confidence interval
   b. 95 percent confidence interval
   c. 99 percent confidence interval
   d. both b and c are correct

_____ 4. The margin of error:

   a. is an acceptable or tolerable range of error in survey research
   b. consists of analyzing the data in order to come to some conclusion or decision
   c. consists of stating quantitatively how much confidence can be placed in the outcome of the research
   d. is always plus or minus three percentage points

_____ 5. The level of error is also referred to as the:

   a. level of significance
   b. alpha level
   c. both a and b
   d. none of the above

_____ 6. If a researcher is 68 percent confident of his or her conclusions, he or she has a _____ chance of being wrong.

   a. 5 percent
   b. 32 percent
   c. 10 percent
   d. 40 percent

_____ 7. If a researcher is 95 percent confident of his or her conclusions he or she has a _____ chance of being wrong?

   a. 5 percent
   b. 32 percent
   c. 10 percent
   d. 40 percent

_____ 8. Nondirectional hypotheses are also referred to as:

   a. one-tailed tests
   b. two-tailed tests
   c. zero-tailed tests
   d. none of the above

_____ 9. If hypotheses have no means present for comparison they are referred to as:

   a. parametric
   b. null hypotheses
   c. nonparametric
   d. none of the above

_____ 10. The confidence interval for criminal trials is:

   a. "proof beyond a reasonable doubt"
   b. "preponderance of the evidence"
   c. both a and b are correct
   d. "clear and convincing evidence"

_____ 11. The *z* test for one-sample means is:

   a. used when a one-sample mean is being compared to some standard or population
   b. a parametric test
   c. a test that requires interval- or ratio-level data
   d. all of the above are correct

True/False Questions

_____ 1. Sampling error can be calculated simply by subtracting the sample mean from the population mean.

_____ 2. A "rule of thumb" in statistics is to use a 68 percent confidence interval.

_____ 3. According to the text, an acceptable margin of error is usually 3 to 5 percent.

_____ 4. Association hypotheses seek to determine if two variables are related to each other.

_____ 5. Association hypotheses are always one-tailed tests.

_____ 6. The confidence interval for criminal trials is "preponderance of the evidence."

_____ 7. If an instructor believes a new teaching method increases final exam scores, that is an example of a directional research hypothesis.

_____ 8. It is more difficult to show a difference than it is to show a direction in statistical testing.

_____ 9. A one-sample z test is useful for examining two characteristics with a single sample.

Essay/Discussion Questions

1. What is statistical significance? Pretend that you are home on semester break and explain it so that your family or friends can understand it.

2. Explain what the term *margin of error* means. How is it related to sample size? What would the margin of error be if the sample size were 1,000?

_____

_____

_____

_____

_____

_____

_____

_____

_____

_____

_____

_____

_____

_____

_____

_____

_____

3. What is the value of calculating z scores? What do z scores tell us?

_____

_____

_____

_____

_____

_____

_____

_____

_____

_____

_____

_____

_____

_____

_____

_____

t Tests and Nonparametric Alternatives

KEY TERMS

chi-square one-sample median test
degrees of freedom
homogeneity
Mann-Whitney *U* test for two independent
    samples
matched-samples *t* test

nonparametric statistics
t test
t test for one-sample means
t test for two independent samples
Wilcoxon matched-pairs signed-ranks test

CHAPTER SUMMARY

I. Introduction

The *t* distribution is ideal when dealing with sample sizes that are smaller than 100.

A *t* test is determined by degrees of freedom; the greater the degrees of freedom, the closer the *t* distribution gets to the normal distribution. However, when the degrees are small, the proportion of the area in the tails is greater than it would be in the normal distribution. Thus, the probability or error is greater when dealing with smaller samples.

II. Degrees of Freedom

These are calculated as $N - 1$, where N is the sample size.

III. t Distribution Table

When you look at a t distribution table (see Appendix B of the textbook), note the difference from a normal distribution table. The left column displays degrees of freedom and there are columns for one-tailed and two-tailed tests. (Level of significance is doubled for the two-tailed test so you do not have to calculate the areas beyond it.)

IV. t Test for One-Sample Means

The steps:

Suppose we have a group of 20 criminology students taking a test one semester. In the previous semester, the class average was 75 percent and the instructor wants to ascertain whether her latter class scored better grades on the final. The grades on the final for the second semester class are as follows:

63, 68, 77, 70, 81, 85, 90, 93, 96, 55, 61, 74, 77, 79, 81, 85, 68, 68, 90, 70

1.   State the hypothesis

$H_o = \mu = 75$

$H_a = \mu \neq 75$

This is for a two-tailed test.

Thus, the null hypothesis states that there will be no significant difference in the average of this semester in comparison to last semester. The alternative or research hypothesis states that there will be a significant difference between the two class averages.

2.   Arrange the data in a frequency table to determine the mean, standard deviation and the standard error of the mean.

test	frequency (f)	fx	x^2	$f(x^2)$
55	1	55	3,025	3,025
61	1	61	3,721	3,721
63	1	63	3,969	3,969
68	3	204	4,624	13,872
70	2	140	4,900	9,800
74	1	74	5,476	5,476
77	2	154	5,929	11,858
79	1	79	6,241	6,241
81	2	162	6,561	13,122
85	2	170	7,225	14,450
90	2	180	8,100	16,200
93	1	93	8,649	8,649
96	1	96	9,216	9,216

$N = 20$ $\Sigma fx = 1,531$ $\Sigma fx^2 = 77,636$ $\Sigma f(x^2) = 119,599$

$$\text{mean } (\overline{X}) \quad = \quad \frac{\Sigma f x}{N} \qquad \frac{1{,}531}{20} \quad = \quad 76.55$$

$$\text{standard deviation} = \sigma \quad = \quad \sqrt{(\Sigma f(x^2) / N) - \overline{X}^2}$$

$$= \quad \sqrt{\frac{119{,}599 - 76.55^2}{20}}$$

$$= \quad \sqrt{5{,}979.95 - 5{,}859.9}$$

$$= \quad \sqrt{120.05}$$

$$\sigma \quad = \quad 10.96$$

The standard error of the mean is calculated as:

$$SE \quad = \quad \frac{\sigma}{\sqrt{N-1}}$$

$$SE \quad = \quad \frac{10.96}{4.35}$$

$$SE \quad = \quad 2.51$$

Then calculate the *t* statistic:

$$t \quad = \quad \frac{\overline{X} - \mu}{SE}$$

$$t \quad = \quad \frac{76.55 - 75}{2.51}$$

$$t \quad = \quad 0.62$$

Calculate the degrees of freedom:

$$df = N - 1$$
$$df = 20 - 1 = 19$$

Now consult the *t* distribution table (see Appendix B of the textbook).

V. *t* Test for Two Independent Samples

To use the *t* test for two independent samples, the two samples must be random and normally distributed; the dependent variable must be at the interval or ratio level; and the two samples must be homogeneous (variances are equal). Go through the same procedure as we did with one sample. However, in this hypothetical example, we will increase our sample sizes to 31 and 30. The first semester mean was 75, with a standard deviation of 12.3 and a sample size of 31; the second semester mean was 76.55, with a standard deviation of 10.96 and a sample size of 30.

Obtain the pooled estimate of the standard deviation (σ_p) for both groups:

$$\sigma_p = \sqrt{[(N_1 \times \sigma_1^2) + (N_2 \times \sigma_2^2)] / (N_1 + N_2)}$$

Where: N_1 = sample size for group 1

N_2 = sample size for group 2

σ_1^2 = standard deviation for group 1, squared

σ_2^2 = standard deviation for group 2, squared

$$\sigma_p = \sqrt{\frac{(31 \times 151.3 + (30 \times 120.12)}{31 + 30}}$$

$$= \sqrt{\frac{4,690.3 + 3,603.6}{61}}$$

$$= \sqrt{135.96}$$

$$\sigma_p = 11.66$$

Next, compute the standard error of the mean:

$$SE = \sigma_p \times \sqrt{[1/(N_1 - 1)] + [1/(N_2 - 1)]}$$

$$SE = 11.66 \times \sqrt{1/30 + 1/29}$$

$$= 11.66 \times \sqrt{0.033 + 0.034}$$

$$= 11.66 \times 0.25$$

$$SE = 2.91$$

Then we compute the t statistic:

$$t = \frac{\overline{X}_1 - \overline{X}_2}{SE}$$

$$t = \frac{76.55 - 75}{2.91}$$

$$t = 0.53$$

Lastly, calculate the degrees of freedom.

$$df = (N_1 + N_2) - 2$$

In our example, the degrees of freedom are $df = (31 + 30) - 2 = 61 - 2 = 59$.

Now consult the t distribution table (see Appendix B of the textbook). If the table does not show the degree of freedom that you need, take the next lowest degree of freedom. In our case we would use 40 degrees of freedom at the 0.05 level of significance; this value is 2.021. Our calculated t statistic was 0.53, so there is no significant difference. We would have to have had a t statistic of at least 2.021 or more at 40 degrees of freedom in order to show a significant difference at the 0.05 level.

VI. Matched-Samples *t* Test

The matched-samples *t* test is used when we have one sample being measured twice. Most often it is a situation involving a before/after type scenario. First, we set up a frequency table with columns for each sample score, as we did in our previous example. Then we compute the standard deviation for the change between scores (time 1 measure minus time 2 measure).

Suppose we were interested in determining if a difference existed between scores on a before and after test with five students:

Student	Before X_1	After X_2	Change $(X_1 - X_2)$	Change $(C)^2$
1	3	6	−3	9
2	4	7	−3	9
3	9	10	−1	1
4	7	9	−2	4
5	5	8	−3	9
	$\overline{X}_1 = 5.6$	$\overline{X}_2 = 8$		$\Sigma C^2 = 32$

Compute the standard deviation of the change.

$$\sigma_c = \sqrt{(\Sigma C^2/N) - (\overline{X}_1 - \overline{X}_2)^2}$$

$$\sigma_c = \sqrt{(32/5) - (5.6 - 8)^2}$$

$$= \sqrt{6.4 - 5.76}$$

$$= \sqrt{.64}$$

$$\sigma_c = .80$$

Then compute the standard error of the mean difference (*SE*) and your *t* statistic.

$$SE_c = \frac{\sigma_c}{\sqrt{N-1}}$$

$$SE_c = \frac{.80}{\sqrt{5-1}}$$

$$= \frac{.80}{\sqrt{4}}$$

$$SE_c = .4$$

$$t = \frac{\overline{X}_1 - \overline{X}_2}{SE}$$

$$t = \frac{5.6 - 8}{.4}$$

$$t = -6.00$$

The degrees of freedom are calculated as $N - 1$.
In our example, $5 - 1 = 4$ degrees of freedom.

* The *t* test can be used anytime that a *z* test is used. It is better for use with smaller samples (i.e., sample sizes under 100).

VII. Alternatives to the *t* Test (Nonparametric Tests)

A. *One-sample median test (chi-square):* The one-sample median (chi-square) test compares expected frequencies with observed frequencies and is designed to determine whether an observed frequency distribution is significantly different from an expected frequency distribution. It is used when data are skewed or when the median describes the data more accurately than does the mean.

The null hypothesis becomes:
H_o = observed median is equal to the expected median.
H_a = observed median is not the same as the expected median.

The formula for computing chi-square is:

$$\chi^2 \quad = \quad \frac{\Sigma\,(o - e)^2}{e}$$

That is, the sum of the observed frequency (*o*) minus the expected frequency (*e*) squared, divided by the expected frequency (*e*). The degrees of freedom: are always equal to 1 for the chi-square median test.

After calculating the chi-square statistic, look at the chi-square table (see Appendix B of the textbook) to find the chi-square value. If the calculated statistic is equal to or larger than the table chi-square value, it is significant at that level of error.

B. *Mann-Whitney U Test for Two Independent Samples:* The Mann-Whitney *U* test for two independent samples is used to test whether two samples are likely to have been drawn from the same distribution. The null hypothesis would state that the two samples have the same distribution (equal medians). First, separate the samples by calling N_1 the smaller sample N_1 and N_2 the larger (even if they are the same number). Then combine the samples and rank them from lowest to highest. If ranks are tied, take the average of the tied position, then plug the information into the following two formulas:

Formula 1: $U \;=\; N_1 N_2 + [N_1(N_1 + 1) / 2] - \Sigma R_1$
Formula 2: $U' \;=\; N_1 N_2 + [N_2(N_2 + 1) / 2] - \Sigma R_2$

Where: N_1 = size of the smaller sample
N_2 = size of the larger sample
ΣR_1 = sum of the ranks for the smaller sample
ΣR_2 = sum of the ranks for the larger sample

The smaller value of *U* is the *U* statistic (either *U* or *U'*). Look on the *U* test table (see Appendix B of the textbook) and find the *U* value that coincides with your sample sizes N_1 and N_2. If the calculated *U* statistic is equal to or less than the tabled *U* value, it is significant at that level of error. The test can be either one-tailed or two-tailed.

C. *Wilcoxon Matched-Pairs Signed-Ranks Test:* The Wilcoxon test (*T*) is the nonparametric equivalent for the *t* test for matched samples. When the researcher has pairs of observations that are measured on at least an ordinal scale, the Wilcoxon test can be used to determine whether there are significant differences between pairs of observations.

As with the *t* test for matched samples, a difference (change) between each pair of observations is calculated. Each of the difference "scores" are then ranked without regard to the sign of the value (negative or positive). The smallest difference is given the rank of 1, the next smallest the rank of 2, and so on. Once ranked, the sign of the differences (negative or positive) is assigned to the ranks. The Wilcoxon statistic (*T*) is calculated by determining the smaller of the sums of ranks (negatives and positives). A Wilcoxon table is consulted (see Appendix B of the textbook) and if a calculated *T* statistic is less than or equal to the value of *T* given in the table for a given significance level, the null hypothesis is rejected. The test can be either one-tailed or two-tailed.

EXERCISES

Short-Answer Questions

1. Conduct a one-sample t test with the following group of scores. Use a "standard" mean of 5 for your comparison (H_o: $\mu = 5$).

    10
    9
    9
    7
    6
    6
    5

    What are your conclusions at the .05 level of significance (two-tailed test)?

2. Conduct a two-sample independent *t* test with the following group of scores (H_o: $\mu_1 = \mu_2$).

X_1	X_2
100	100
100	90
95	88
90	80
90	75
88	75
87	70

What are your conclusions at the .05 level of significance (two-tailed test)?

3.   Conduct a matched sample t test with the following before/after scores (H_o: $\mu_1 = \mu_2$).

Before	After
10	5
9	4
8	6
8	6
7	3

What are your conclusions at the .05 level of significance (two-tailed test)?

4. Using the data in problem 1, conduct a one-sample median test (chi-square) using a "standard" median of 5. What are your conclusions at the .05 level of significance?

5. Using the data in problem 2, conduct a Mann-Whitney *U* test. What are your conclusions at the .05 level of significance?

6. Using the data in problem 3, conduct a Wilcoxon Matched-Pairs Signed-Ranks Test. What are your conclusions at the .05 level of significance?

Multiple-Choice Questions

_____ 1. The definition of "degrees of freedom" is:

   a. the number of values of the variable that are free to vary
   b. calculated as $N - 1$
   c. a nonparametric equivalent of the t test
   d. both a and b are correct

_____ 2. It is appropriate to use the t test for two independent samples when:

   a. two random samples are drawn from two normally distributed populations under study
   b. the dependent variable is measured at the interval or ratio level of measurement
   c. the two samples are homogeneous
   d. all of the above are correct

_____ 3. Homogeneity refers to the:

   a. "equalness" of the variances between two samples
   b. "unequalness" of the variances between the two samples
   c. "unequalness" of the means between the two samples
   d. "equalness" of the means between the two samples

_____ 4. A good rule to follow when using the *t* table that does not show the actual degree of freedom that you need is to:

    a. take the next highest degree of freedom value
    b. stop working the problem because it cannot be solved
    c. take the next lowest degree of freedom
    d. none of the above are correct

_____ 5. The *t* test can:

    a. be used anytime that a *z* test can be used
    b. be used for small samples under 100
    c. be used for small samples under 30 if the researcher can assume the sample is normally distributed and not skewed
    d. all of the above are correct

_____ 6. The *t* test should only be used with what type of data?

    a. nominal/ordinal data
    b. interval/ratio data
    c. nominal/ratio data
    d. ordinal/interval data

_____ 7. Nominal and ordinal data must be tested using:

    a. nonparametric statistics
    b. parametric statistics
    c. distribution-free statistics
    d. both a and c are correct

_____ 8. The chi-square median test uses the _____ of a data set rather than the mean.

    a. mode
    b. median
    c. average
    d. none of the above are correct

_____ 9. The Wilcoxon Matched-Pairs Signed-Ranks Test is:

    a. the nonparametric equivalent of the *t* test for matched samples
    b. the nonparametric equivalent to the independent groups *t* test
    c. both a and b are correct
    d. none of the above are correct

_____ 10. As the degrees of freedom increase in the *t* distribution, the *t* value marking the boundary for a particular level of error

    a. increases
    b. decreases
    c. remains the same
    d. becomes skewed

True/False Questions

_____ 1. The normal (z) distribution has been proven to be inappropriate for use with smaller samples.

_____ 2. Degrees of freedom is a concept closely related to sample size.

_____ 3. The t distribution is identical to the normal (z) distribution when the degrees of freedom go over 50.

_____ 4. The curve for a t distribution is "plumper" in extreme regions of the tails and flatter in the central area.

_____ 5. Degrees of freedom refers to the number of values of the variable that are not free to vary.

_____ 6. You will see degrees of freedom being calculated as $N - 10$.

_____ 7. Larger sample sizes (over 100) are more normally distributed.

_____ 8. Homogeneity refers to the "unequalness" of the variances between the two samples.

_____ 9. When using the t table that does not show the actual degrees of freedom you need, then take the next lowest degree of freedom value.

_____ 10. A t test can be used for samples under 30 if the researcher can assume the sample is normally distributed and not skewed.

_____ 11. The t test should be used only with nominal or ordinal measures.

_____ 12. The chi-square median test uses the median of a data set rather than the mean.

_____ 13. Nonparametric tests are not as "powerful" as parametric tests.

13 Analysis of Variance

KEY TERMS

analysis of variance (ANOVA)
between-groups variation
column null hypothesis (H_a)
ex post facto research
F distribution
factorial design
Friedman two-way ANOVA
interaction
Kruskal-Wallis one-way ANOVA

one-way ANOVA for independent samples
one-way ANOVA for repeated measures
robustness
row null hypothesis (H_o)
Scheffé test
total variation
Tukey's honestly significant difference
    (HSD) test
within-group variation

CHAPTER SUMMARY

I. Introduction

Analysis of variance (ANOVA) is a technique specifically designed to handle the comparison of means from more than two groups (in the case of independent samples) or more than two measures (as in the case of matched samples).

II. Function of ANOVA

One-way ANOVA for independent groups is used for testing the hypothesis that three or more independent samples were drawn from populations having the same mean. There is a second approach known as the *ex post facto design* that takes three random samples from three populations. Each population would have to have an independent variable. This method helps to increase the chances of obtaining representative samples.

A. *Rationale of ANOVA:* ANOVA techniques are designed to treat all data at once with a null hypothesis of no differences among the means. Thus, ANOVA is a one-directional test. There can be two types of one-directional tests: *between-groups variation* and *within-group variation*. If all scores from all groups are lumped together, these combined scores would be referred to as total variation. ANOVA can be used when: (1) the dependent variable is measured on an interval or ratio level, (2) units of analysis (subjects or scores) have been selected on the basis of random sampling, and (3) the variance of the groups are homogeneous (equal or nearly equal).

   ANOVA is "robust," which means that as a statistical test it is accurate even with minor violations of homogeneity and normally distributed populations. ANOVA is similar to the *t* test but ANOVA works with variances rather than standard deviations. ANOVA uses two types of degrees of freedom: between-groups degrees of freedom and within-group degrees of freedom. The *t* distribution uses within-groups only since there are only one of two samples with which to work. Thus, ANOVA has its own distribution table known as the *F* table. The between-groups degrees of freedom is indicated as *df*1 and is the number of groups (K) minus 1. The within-group degrees of freedom (*df*2) is determined by adding the total *N*s in each group and subtracting the between-group degrees of freedom from them ($NT - K$).

   Like the *t* test, if a calculated *F* statistic (ANOVA) equals or exceeds the tabled *F* value, it is significant at that level of error. The square root of an *F* value equals what the *t* value would be. Remember that ANOVA is a nondirectional test only (two-tailed, so any significant difference may be between two of the groups or all of the groups).

III. Step-by-Step Procedure

1. State the hypothesis: The null hypothesis will state that the three or more groups are all equal in mean scores. The research hypothesis will state that the means are not equal.

2. Organize the data.

3. Find the total sum of squares by:

$$SST = \Sigma X^2 T - [(\Sigma XT)^2 / NT]$$ Where: SST = Sum of Squares Total

$$\Sigma X^2 T = \Sigma X^2_1 + \Sigma X^2_2 + \Sigma X^2_3$$

$$\Sigma XT = \Sigma X_1 + \Sigma X_2 + \Sigma X_3$$

$$NT = \text{total } N \ (N_1 + N_2 + N_3)$$

4. Find the between-groups sum of squares by:

$$SSB = (\Sigma[(\Sigma X)^2 / N]) - [(\Sigma XT)^2 / N]$$ Where: SSB = Sum of Squares Between
$(\Sigma X)^2$ = sum of scores for *each* group, squared
$(\Sigma XT)^2 = (\Sigma X_1 + \Sigma X_2 + \Sigma X_3)^2$

5. Determine the within-group sum of squares by:

$$SSW = SST - SSB$$ Where: SSW = Sum of Squares Within
SST = Sum of Squares Total
SSB = Sum of Squares Between

6. Find the degrees of freedom, first the between-groups (*dfb*) and then the within-groups (*dfw*):

$$dfb = K - 1 \qquad \text{Where:} \quad K = \text{Number of Groups}$$

$$dfw = NT - K \qquad \text{Where:} \quad NT = N_1 + N_2 + N_3$$
$$K = \text{Number of Groups}$$

7. Calculate the between-groups mean square:

$$MSB = SSB / dfb$$

8. Calculate the within-group mean square:

$$MSW = SSW / dfw$$

9. Obtain the *F* statistic:

$$F = MSB / MSW$$

10. Compare the calculated *F* statistic to the tabled *F* value. See Appendix B of the textbook.

IV. Comparing the Means

If the null hypothesis of no difference is rejected by ANOVA, it is reasonable to assume that at least one sample mean differs significantly from another sample mean. If all the samples are of equal size, the researcher may conclude that the largest mean is significantly larger than the smallest mean. Thus, one would test those two groups further.

V. Multiple-Comparison Means Tests

Multiple-comparison means tests are used only if the ANOVA (*F*) is found to be significant (i.e., it rejects the null hypothesis).

A. *Scheffé test:* The Scheffé test is not limited to samples of equal size. It compares two means at a time, but takes into account the number of groups under study by ANOVA. The Scheffé test formula for testing any and all possible comparisons between means is:

$$F = (\bar{X}_1 - \bar{X}_2)^2 / MSW (1 / N_1 + 1 / N_2) (K - 1)$$

Again, find the degrees of freedom by $df1 = K - 1$ and $df2 = N - K$

B. *Tukey's Honestly Significant Difference (HSD) Test:* Tukey's HSD test can be used in all single pairwise comparisons when the samples are of equal size.

$$HSD = q \sqrt{MSW / N}$$

$$\text{Where:} \quad q = \frac{\bar{X}_1 - \bar{X}_2}{\sqrt{MSW/N}}$$

1. Set up a table of difference between ordered means, from smallest to largest. Work out the difference between the means and put them in the table.

2. Find q by examining Appendix B, Table 8 of the textbook.

3. Calculate HSD and compare it to the table of differences we constructed in step 1. To be statistically significant at the 0.05 level, any obtained mean difference in the table must equal or exceed the HSD statistic.

These two multiple comparison tests can only be used with independent group means. When the groups are matched, such as in repeated measures with one group, neither the Scheffé test nor Tukey's HSD should be used.

VI. Repeated-Measures ANOVA

Repeated-measures ANOVA is used when one sample is measured three or more times. The design is referred to as repeated measures, within subjects or matched samples. The null hypothesis would state that there is no difference between the means in the scores.

Calculating a repeated-measures ANOVA by hand is a time-consuming process. It is strongly recommended that a computer statistical program such as SPSS be used instead. See the computer illustration in the text.

VII. Nonparametric Alternatives to ANOVA

Nonparametric alternatives to ANOVA are used when sample sizes are too small (under 30), when data are severely skewed, or when the data are measured at the ordinal level.

A. *Kruskal-Wallis (K-W) one-way ANOVA:* Kruskal-Wallis (K-W) one-way ANOVA is used in determining if K independent samples (more than two) were likely to have been drawn from the same population. The dependent variable must be measured on at least the ordinal level. In the K-W ANOVA, each of the observations are replaced by ranks like the procedure for the Mann-Whitney U test in Chapter 12. If the sums of the group ranks are sufficiently close to one another, the researcher can conclude that the samples came from the same population (thus, the null hypothesis is true). If the null hypothesis is true and the groups came from the same population, then the K-W statistic will be distributed the same as the chi-square distribution ($df = K - 1$). If there are five or more cases in each of the groups, then the chi-square distribution can be used. As with the chi-square one-sample median test, if the H statistic is equal to or greater than the chi-square tabled value, it is significant at that level of error and the null hypothesis can be rejected.

B. *Friedman two-way ANOVA for repeated measures*: The Friedman two-way ANOVA for repeated measures is used to test the null hypothesis that the samples (K) have been drawn from the same population. Again the samples must at least be measured on the ordinal level. This test can be viewed as an extension of the Wilcoxon matched-pairs signed-ranks test discussed in chapter 12. The data are set up as a two-way table having rows and columns. The rows equal the number of subjects; the columns equal the number of measures or treatments. To test the difference in rank totals, the Friedman test requires that a special statistic be calculated. The statistic is denoted as X_{x2} and is calculated as:

$$X_r^2 = 12 / N_K(K + 1) \sum(R_j)^2 - 3N(K + 1)$$ Where:

N =	number of observations or rows
K =	number of columns or measurements
R_j =	sum of the ranks in each column

If the calculated statistic is equal to or greater than the tabled chi-squared value, the null hypothesis can be rejected at that level of error.

VIII. Two-way ANOVA: Factorial Design

One-way ANOVA and its nonparametric counterparts are used to test the hypothesis that three or more groups have the same population mean. There can be one treatment variable (the independent variable). For example, one could use an intoxication level that has several different levels: sober, slightly affected and intoxicated. It is also possible to design experiments that have a two-way design or two independent variables. This is done with two-way ANOVA, which tests two hypotheses at the same time and also tests the null hypothesis to determine whether there is interaction between the two independent variables. *Interaction* refers to when the effectiveness of one independent variable depends on the level of the other independent variable. Thus, there are three null hypotheses that can be tested with two-way ANOVA: (1) the null hypothesis for columns, (2) the null hypothesis for rows, and (3) the interaction of rows with columns. Each null hypothesis is tested by ANOVA with its own F value.

Degrees of freedom are calculated for a two-way ANOVA by determining the number of cells in the factorial design, the number of scores in each cell and the number of rows and columns in the design. The degrees of freedom within each cell is $rc(n-1)$ and the row degrees of freedom is calculated by $r - 1$.

EXERCISES

Short-Answer Questions

1. Test for the significance of differences among means of the following scores:

X_1	X_2	X_3	X_4
7	3	4	3
6	4	5	4
5	3	3	2
8	4	3	3
8	6	5	3

What are your conclusions for the .05 level of significance?

2. Conduct a multiple comparison of means using Tukey's HSD test to determine exactly where the significant differences occur in problem 1. What are your conclusions?

3. Conduct a Kruskal-Wallis one-way ANOVA for the data in problem 1. What are your conclusions for the .05 level of significance?

4. Five persons were tested on three different occasions. Test for the difference between means using repeated-measures ANOVA.

Subject	Test 1	Test 2	Test 3
1	10	8	7
2	8	5	4
3	10	5	4
4	7	4	3
5	8	6	5

What are your conclusions for the .05 level of significance?

5. Conduct a Friedman two-way ANOVA for repeated measures in problem 4. What are your conclusions for the .05 level of significance?

Multiple-Choice Questions

_____ 1. Analysis of variance is a statistical technique specifically designed to handle the comparison of means from:

    a. more than two groups
    b. more than two measures
    c. both a and c are correct
    d. none of the above are correct

_____ 2. One-way ANOVA for independent groups is used for:

    a. testing the hypothesis that two independent samples were drawn from populations having the same mean
    b. testing the hypothesis that three or more independent samples were drawn from populations having the same mean
    c. testing whether x causes y
    d. none of the above are correct

_____ 3. In one-way ANOVA we are concerned with what type(s) of variation?

    a. between-groups variation
    b. within-group variation
    c. both a and c are correct
    d. none of the above is correct

_____ 4. Between-groups variation refers to:

    a. variation of group means
    b. variation of the scores within each group
    c. variation in the standard deviations of the group
    d. variation in the robustness of the group

_____ 5. Within-group variation refers to:

    a. variation of group means
    b. variation of the scores within each group
    c. variation in the standard deviations of the group
    d. variations in the robustness of the group

_____ 6. ANOVA can be used when the following condition(s) are met:

    a. the dependent variable is measured at interval or ratio level
    b. the units of analysis in the various groups have been selected on the basis of random sampling
    c. the variance of the groups is homogenous
    d. all of the above are correct

_____ 7. What type(s) of degrees of freedom does ANOVA use?

    a. between-groups degrees of freedom
    b. within-group degrees of freedom
    c. both a and b are correct
    d. none of the above

_____ 8. Which of the following is/are true for the Scheffé test?

    a. It is not limited to samples of equal size
    b. It provides a calculated F statistic that can be compared to the F table
    c. It compares two means at a time
    d. It takes into account the number of groups under study by ANOVA

_____ 9. Interaction refers to:

    a. when the effectiveness of one independent variable depends on the level of the other independent variable
    b. when three or more group means are being contrasted
    c. the variance of the groups
    d. none of the above

True/False Questions

_____ 1. When three or more group means are being contrasted, the t test is no longer valid.

_____ 2. In one-way ANOVA we are concerned with between-groups variation and outside-groups variation.

_____ 3. Variation of the scores within each group is referred to as between-groups variation.

_____ 4. Variation of group means is referred to as between-groups variation.

_____ 5. Robustness indicates that the test is accurate even with minor violations of homogeneity and normally distributed populations.

_____ 6. ANOVA is a one-tailed directional test.

_____ 7. The Scheffé test or Tukey's HSD test can be used when the sample sizes are unequal.

_____ 8. The Scheffé test and Tukey's HSD test can be used only with independent groups.

_____ 9. The Kruskal-Wallis test is a nonparametric alternative to one-way analysis of variance for independent groups.

_____ 10. The Friedman two-way ANOVA for repeated measures is a nonparametric alternative to the ANOVA with repeated measures.

_____ 11. Interaction refers to when the effectiveness of one dependent variable depends on the level of the other dependent variable.

14

Correlation and Regression Analysis

KEY TERMS

bivariate relationships
causation
coefficient of determination
coefficient of nondetermination
correlation
dummy variable
Goodman's and Kruskal's gamma
Kendall's tau
multiple regression
negative/inverse relationship

outliers
partial correlation
Pearson's r
positive/direct relationship
regression
scatterplots
Spearman's rho
spurious relationship
temporal priority

CHAPTER SUMMARY

I. Introduction

X = independent variable measured at interval or ratio level.
Y = dependent variable measured at interval or ratio level.

If X and Y vary together, then they are correlated. If it can be proven that X preceded Y in time, then we can say X causes Y (in the absence of other variables).

II. Types of Relationships

A. *Positive or direct relationship:* if X and Y both increase or decrease together.

B. *Negative or inverse relationship*: if one increases and the other decreases.

Causation exists when the following are true:

1. *X* and *Y* must vary together.

2. The cause (*X*) must precede the effect (*Y*) in time (temporal priority).

3. There must be no other variables influencing *X* or *Y*, if there are, then the relationship between *X* and *Y* is considered to be *spurious*.

III. Scatterplots

In a scatterplot one can view the possible correlation by plotting *X* against *Y*. Draw a line through the points that best fits all the points (the *best-fitting line*) to establish whether there is a positive or inverse relationship. If no line fits the data, the relationship may be curvilinear and thus cannot be correlated in a linear fashion. *Outliers* in scatterplots are those extreme values that can dramatically affect statistics (e.g., the mean). You may want to exclude these from your data set to give a more accurate analysis of your data. However, any outliers that are excluded must be reported.

IV. Pearson's Correlation Coefficient (*r*)

Pearson's *r* measures a linear (straight-line) relationship between two variables. It ranges from –1 to +1. An *r* value of +1 indicates a perfect positive relationship (this rarely happens). If no relationship exists, Pearson's *r* takes a value of 0. The closer the value of the coefficient is to –1 or +1, the stronger the relationship.

The formula for calculating Pearson's *r:*

$$r = \frac{\Sigma XY - N(\overline{X})(\overline{Y})}{\sqrt{[\Sigma X^2 - N(\overline{X})^2]\ [\Sigma Y^2 - N(\overline{Y})^2]}}$$

V. Coefficient of Determination

To obtain this value, we square the coefficient to r^2. This then expresses the percentage or proportion of variability in the dependent variable (*Y*) that is explained by its association with the independent variable (*X*). For example, suppose we obtain a Pearson's *r* of 0.66 (the correlation between *X* and *Y*), then $r^2 =$ 0.436. This indicates that 43.6 percent of the variability in *Y* can be explained by its relationship to the independent variable *X*. The compliment of r^2 ($1 - r^2$) explains the proportion of variance in the *Y* variable that is *not* explained by its relationship to the *X* variable. This is called the *coefficient of nondetermination*.

VI. Testing the Significance of Pearson's *r*

The null hypothesis states that a calculated correlation is not significantly different from zero. The *t* distribution is skewed, the degrees of freedom are calculated as two less than the number of pairs of observations (*N* – 2). The formula for calculating the *t* value of a correlation coefficient (*r*) is:

$$t \quad = \quad r / \sqrt{(1 - r^2) / N - 2} \qquad \text{Where:} \quad r \; = \; \text{the calculated correlation coefficient}$$
$$N \; = \; \text{the sample size}$$

The calculated t value is then compared to the t distribution table in the same manner as any other calculated t statistic. If you are comparing a negative value, focus on its absolute value rather than the actual integer (e.g., the absolute value of –3 is 3).

VII. Partial Correlation

Often a correlation between two variables ignores the influence of a third or other variables. Partial correlation helps control for the effects of third variables on the original correlation between the two variables X and Y.

Step-by-Step Procedure

Suppose we have two variables: juveniles that come from broken homes (X) and the juvenile crime rate (Y). A possible third variable that may influence these two is years of education (Z). Suppose the correlation between X and Y is determined to be 0.48 (r_{xy}). We then have to calculate the correlation coefficient of both variables X and Y with Z. If the correlation coefficient for number of years of education and crime rate is 0.51 (r_{xz}) and the correlation coefficient for number of years of education and broken homes is 0.38 (r_{zy}), the partial correlation can be calculated from the following formula:

$$r_{xy \cdot z} \quad = \quad \frac{r_{xy} - (r_{xz})\,(r_{yz})}{\sqrt{1 - (r_{xz})^2} \;\; \sqrt{1 - (r_{yz})^2}}$$

In this case:

$$r_{xy \cdot z} \quad = \quad \frac{0.48 \; - \; (0.38)(0.51)}{\sqrt{0.77} \quad \times \quad \sqrt{0.74}}$$

$$= \quad \frac{0.48 - 0.1938}{0.88 \; \times \; 0.86}$$

$$= \quad \frac{0.286}{0.757}$$

$$r_{xy \cdot z} \quad = \quad 0.38$$

Interpreting $r_{xy \cdot z}$: An $r_{xy \cdot z}$ of 0.38 may be interpreted as a moderate correlation. Thus, when we control for the effects of education, there is a moderate correlation between juveniles who come from broken homes and juvenile crime rates.

VIII. Alternative Nonparametric Tests

When the requirements for Pearson's r are not met (e.g., if the variables are not measured on an interval or ratio level or the sample size is too small), there are nonparametric alternatives.

A. *Spearman's rho:* Spearman's rho is used for ranked data (ordinal) and where the sample size is less than 30. It is interpreted the same way as Pearson's r. For example, if we have a survey that requires officers to rank five offenses in order of seriousness (1 being the most serious), the dependent variable (*Y*) would be the seriousness of the offense and the independent (*X*) variable could be the years of experience the officer has.

1. State the null hypothesis: there is no relationship between the years of experience an officer has and how they rank serious offenses.

2. Rank the data:

Subject	Y	X (Years of experience)	Y Rank (most serious offense)
1	12	5	1.8
2	11	5	1.8
3	8	3	2.6
4	6	2	9.5
5	5	3	2.6
6	4	5	1.8
7	2	2	9.5
8	1	2	9.5

If two or more subjects are tied in the ranking process, the mean of the positions is taken. For example, all eight subjects have ties with the *Y* variable, so the *Y* variable column is displayed as shown in the final right hand column. For example, subjects 4, 7 and 8 have 2 as the most serious offense. We add 4 + 7 + 8 and divide by 2, which equals 9.5.

Rho is calculated by:

$$\text{rho } (\rho) \ = \ 1 - 6\Sigma D^2 \ / \ N(N^2 - 1) \qquad \text{Where: } D^2 = \text{difference in rank between } X \text{ and } Y \text{ squared}$$
$$N = \text{total number of cases or subjects}$$

To test the significance of rho, consult the rho table (see Appendix B of the textbook). If our computed rho value exceeds the table value, the null hypothesis is rejected at that level of significance.

B. *Kendall's Tau and Goodman's and Kruskal's Gamma:* Kendall's tau is often used in place of rho, but it is more difficult to calculate. Goodman's and Kruskal's gamma can also be used in place of rho, especially in crosstabulations or in contingency table analysis with ordinal data.

IX. Regression Analysis

A. *Regression Analysis:* Regression analysis enables us to explain how much change in a dependent variable (*Y*) is associated with a one-unit change in an independent variable (*X*). The equation for a straight line is:

$$Y = a + bX + e$$

Y = a function of some constant (*a*), a multiplier of *X*(*b*) and an error term (*e*). The constant (or *Y* intercept) is the point at which the line will cross the *Y*-axis. The multiplier, *b*, is the regression coefficient. It shows how much change there is in *Y* for every one unit change in *X*. The error term, *e*, represents the fact that we have sampling error in our observations. The presence of error does not enter into our actual calculations of the equation. Regression analysis is concerned with certain properties of the straight line itself. The height of the line is determined by *a* and the steepness of the line is determined by *b*.

X. Calculating the Regression Equation

1.   The basic formula for calculating the steepness (*b*) is as follows:

$$b = \frac{\sum(X - \overline{X})(Y - \overline{Y})}{\sum(X - \overline{X})^2}$$

The computational formula for *b* is:

$$b = \frac{\sum XY - N(\overline{X})(\overline{Y})}{\sum X^2 - N(\overline{X})^2}$$

The formula for calculating the height (*a*) is:

$$a = Y - b\overline{X}$$

After you plug your data into these formulas, plot the regression line on a scatterplot by simply plotting two points on the line, the *Y*-intercept (*a*) and a value of *X* determined by the regression equation.

We can predict the values of *Y* from the regression equation. For example, suppose our equation has been determined as:

$$Y = 64.93 + 0.635(X)$$

Then, what will the value of *Y* be if *X* = 19.5?

Simply plug this data into the line equation so that we have:

$$
\begin{aligned}
Y &= 64.93 + 0.635(19.5) \\
&= 64.93 + 12.382 \\
&= 77.31
\end{aligned}
$$

Note: The main difference between regression and correlation is that correlation is symmetrical (i.e., if the correlation between *X* and *Y* is 0.5, then the correlation between *Y* and *X* is also symmetrical). Regression is not symmetrical. Correlation is also scale-free while regression is not.

XI. Uses of Correlation and Regression

Both correlation and regression are used often for recidivism research. Regression is also used for studying impacts of variables, such as race, on outcomes of the criminal justice system, such as sentencing patterns.

XII. The Dummy Variable

A dummy variable is used in calculating regression for variables not measured at the interval or ratio level. Researchers transpose variables that are measured at the nominal or ordinal level to the interval or ratio level by assigning them a number. For example, gender is often a dummy variable; the researcher easily transposes this variable to an interval level by assigning males the value of 0 and females the value of 1, or vice versa.

EXERCISES

Short-Answer Questions

Consider the following data:

X	Y
2	4
5	8
1	2
6	10
3	2
4	4
5	5
1	2
5	6
5	7

1. Draw a scatterplot of the data.

2. What is the correlation between *X* and *Y*?

3. Is the correlation statistically significant?

4. Perform a regression analysis on the data in problems 1 through 3. Draw the "best-fitting line" on the scatterplot you drew in problem 1.

5. If $X = 5$, what would you predict Y to be?

Multiple-Choice Questions

_____ 1. If X and Y both increase together or both decrease together then that is called:

    a. a positive relationship
    b. a direct relationship
    c. a negative relationship
    d. an inverse relationship
    e. both a and b are correct

_____ 2. If X increases when Y decreases, that is called:

    a. a positive/direct relationship
    b. a negative/inverse relationship
    c. a and b are correct
    d. none of the above are correct

_____ 3. To establish causation, which of the following condition(s) must be satisfied?

    a. It must be shown that X and Y are correlated
    b. It must be shown that a cause precedes its effect
    c. It is necessary to rule out the possibility that other variables cause both X and Y
    d. all of the above are correct

_____ 4. Temporal priority has to do with:

    a. X preceding Y in time order
    b. the fact that no other antecedent variable better explains Y
    c. which mathematical operation is completed first
    d. none of the above

_____ 5. If a line slopes upward from left to right on a scatterplot then the graph is showing a(n):

    a. negative relationship
    b. inverse relationship
    c. positive relationship
    d. curvilinear relationship

_____ 6. If a line slopes downward from left to right this suggests a:

    a. negative relationship
    b. positive relationship
    c. direct relationship
    d. curvilinear relationship

_____ 7. Pearson's correlation coefficient (r) can range from:

    a. -2.0 to 2.0
    b. -1.0 to 1.0
    c. -3.0 to 3.0
    d. -4.0 to 4.0

_____ 8. When a correlation between two variables is actually caused by a third variable it is known as a:

      a. partial correlation
      b. bivariate relationship
      c. spurious relationship
      d. multivariate relationship

_____ 9. The requirement(s) for the use of Pearson's r is/are:

      a. a straight-line (linear) relationship
      b. interval- or ratio-level data
      c normally distributed data
      d. all of the above

True/False Questions

_____ 1. The independent variable is labeled X.

_____ 2. The dependent variable is labeled Y.

_____ 3. If X and Y both increase together or both decrease together, it is a negative relationship.

_____ 4. If one variable increases and the other decreases, it is an inverse relationship.

_____ 5. Bivariate relationships are relationships between three variables at a time.

_____ 6. The first way to investigate a possible correlation between two variables is by inspecting a scatterplot.

_____ 7. Temporal priority means that no other antecedent variable better explains the dependent variable.

_____ 8. If the line on a scatterplot slopes upward from left to right, the graph is indicating a negative relationship.

_____ 9. If a line on a scatterplot slopes downward from left to right, the graph is indicating a positive relationship.

_____ 10. Pearson's r is a measure of a linear relationship between two variables measured at the interval or ratio level.

_____ 11. An r (Pearson's correlation coefficient) of 1.0 indicates a perfect positive relationship.

_____ 12. The coefficient of determination allows researchers to put the magnitude of a correlation coefficient into a proper perspective.

_____ 13. Regression is symmetrical.

Essay/Discussion Questions

1. Survey research usually takes place at one point in time. If you were conducting a survey of delinquents, how would you design survey questions that would still allow you to address the causation of delinquency?

2. If you had the luxury of unlimited time and resources, what would be the best way to design a study concerning the causes of delinquency? Address the three conditions needed to establish causation.

3. Compare and contrast correlation and causation. Give examples.

4. Discuss the usefulness of scatterplots. What assistance do they offer?

15

Contingency Table Analysis

KEY TERMS

causation
chi square
contingency table
contingency table analysis
correlation
Cramer's *V*

degrees of freedom
lambda
phi
sample statistic
temporal priority
Yates's Correction for Continuity

CHAPTER SUMMARY

I. Introduction

A. Contingency table analysis is an important tool in statistical analysis. Contingency tables can be used with all levels of data. However, chi-square analyses are most commonly used with nominal and ordinal data. Contingency tables allow researchers to examine independent and dependent variables with two or more attributes at once.

B. Contingency tables present frequencies and percentages in tabular format in order to summarize large quantities of data in a small space. An example of a contingency table for an experiment with a simple success/failure design can be set up as follows. First we would define the variables in the experiment. For example, if a group of 100 sex offenders went through an intensive therapy program and a different group of 100 sex offenders went though a regular program, recidivism rates could be measured. Those that did not reoffend are successes and those that do reoffend are failures. Hypothetically, the contingency table could look something like this:

C. Hypothetical results of intensive treatment compared to regular treatment programs.

Type of Program

Recidivism	intensive program		regular program		row totals	
	N	%	N	%	N	%
success	70	70.0	57	57.0	127	63.5
failure	30	30.0	43	43.0	73	36.5
column totals	100	100.0	100	100.0	200	100.0

The independent variable (type of program) is positioned on the table by columns and percentaged to 100 percent. This is to establish causality. The dependent variable (recidivism) is positioned by rows. Because there are two attributes of the independent variable (intensive program and regular program) and there are two attributes of the dependent variable (success and failure), the table is called a 2 x 2 table.

A quick glance at this table would indicate that the intensive program for sex offenders in this experiment has appeared to be more successful than the usual program. The table gives frequency of interest, that is, the number of people in each group and how many succeeded or failed. The table also presents how many offenders succeeded and how many failed after the completion of the program. Thus, a contingency table presents two frequency distributions side by side.

II. Further Analysis

A. If the results were more difficult to interpret (for instance, if the percentages of success and failure were much closer in value for both variables), we would bring in the chi-square test. By applying this test to the given contingency table, we can compute a test statistic that would allow us to see whether there is a significant difference between the percentage of participants in the intensive program who succeeded and the percentage of participants in the regular program who succeeded.

B. The first step is to state the null and the research hypothesis. Then we would calculate the chi-square test statistic and compare the calculated chi-square value with the tabled chi-square value for the particular level of error of interest (see Appendix B of the textbook). If the calculated test statistic equals or exceeds the tabled value, one can conclude that there is a significant difference between the two groups. If the test statistic is smaller than the tabled value, we fail to reject the null hypothesis and infer that there is no difference between the two groups.

C. In order to work with chi-square, we need to calculate expected values for each cell. That is, we must determine what we would expect, according to the laws of probability, to find occurring for each attribute. The formula for this is:

Row Total x Column Total / N

In our table the expected values are as follows:

Success Total (127) times Intensive Total (100) divided by N (200) = 63.5
Success Total (127) times Regular Total (100) divided by N (200) = 63.5
Failure Total (73) times Intensive Total (100) divided by N (200) = 36.5
Failure Total (73) times Regular Total (100) divided by N (200) = 36.5

Therefore, we would expect under probability the following would occur with these totals:

Type of Program

Recidivism	intensive program		regular program		row totals	
	N	%	N	%	N	%
success	63.5	63.5	63.5	63.5	127	63.5
failure	36.5	36.5	36.5	36.5	73	36.5
column totals	100	100.0	100	100.0	200	100.0

D. Then use the chi-square formula by subtracting each expected value from its associated observed value, square the difference and divide by the expected value. After doing all that for each cell in the table, add up the results to obtain the chi-square statistic. For the above example:

$$\chi^2 = \Sigma \frac{(f_o - f_e)^2}{f_e}$$

With our example:

$$\chi^2 = [(70 - 63.5)^2 / 63.5] + [(30 - 36.5)^2 / 36.5] + [(57 - 63.5)^2 / 63.5] + [(43 - 36.5)^2 / 36.5]$$

$$= .67 + 1.16 + .67 + 1.16 = 3.66$$

$$\chi^2 = 3.66$$

Next, determine the degrees of freedom, the formula for this is:

$$df = \text{(number of rows - 1)} \times \text{(number of columns - 1)}$$

$$df = (r - 1)(c - 1)$$

Thus, in our example with a 2 × 2 table, the degrees of freedom are equal to:

$$df = (2 - 1)(2 - 1)$$

$$df = 1$$

E. The final step is to compare the obtained or calculated chi-square statistic (3.66) with the value found in a table of chi-square values (see Appendix B of the textbook). According to the chi-square table, at the .05 level of error for one degree of freedom, the tabled chi-square value is 3.841. Our obtained chi-square statistic was 3.66. The calculated value of 3.66 falls short of the 3.841 for the .05 level of error boundary and is therefore not significant. We would conclude that the intensive program did not significantly differ from the regular program in terms of recidivism with these offenders. We must fail to reject the null hypothesis of no significant difference.

F. Any table that is larger than a 2 × 2 can be analyzed in the same way using the same formula. If an expected value is calculated as less than 5, we need to correct it with Yates's correction. The chi-square formula using Yates's correction is:

$$\chi^2 = \Sigma ([f_o - f_e] - .5)^2 / f_e$$

Yates's correction also should be used when the total sample is less than 100 with 2 × 2 tables.

III. Strength of Relationships

A. Chi-square measures only the significance of a relationship. In order to test the strength of the relationship, a correlation coefficient is used much like Pearson's r for interval- and ratio-level data. Phi is a correlation coefficient statistic that measures the strength of a significant chi-square relationship between two nominal level variables. Phi is used with dichotomous variables (two attributes) or for 2 x 2 tables.

Phi is calculated as:

$$\text{phi } (\phi) \quad = \quad \sqrt{\chi^2 / N}$$

B. If a contingency table has more than two rows or columns, phi is an inappropriate test. Instead one could use Cramer's V, which may be used for any size table (e.g., 2 × 2, 2 × 3, 3 × 3, etc.). Cramer's V is calculated the same as phi, the only difference being that the number of rows and columns is taken into consideration.

The formula for Cramer's V is:

$$V \quad = \quad \sqrt{\chi^2 / N (K - 1)} \qquad \text{Where: } K = \text{Smaller number of rows or columns}$$

C. Both phi and Cramer's V are interpreted the same as other correlation coefficients. The statistic ranges from 1.0 to 0, with larger values indicating greater strength of association between variables. Phi and Cramer's V should be calculated only if a significant chi-square statistic is found. It makes little sense to calculate a strength of a relationship that is found to be insignificant by chi-square.

D. Remember that when using correlation for variables, correlation does not mean causation. First, a significant relationship between the two variables has to be proven, then temporal priority must be established, and lastly extraneous variables that may be influencing the relationship must be excluded. For a review of correlation see chapter 14.

IV. Lambda

Like phi and Cramer's V, lambda is a useful statistic for measuring association between two nominal variables. Lambda may be used in a predictive manner in order to predict one variable when you know the value of another. In this sense, lambda is like regression analysis with nominal data.

Using the example from the textbook, suppose one were interested in examining the relationship between a person's fear of crime and that person's opinion about whether the police are doing a good job. The following data were collected on 150 people:

Fear of Crime

		Yes		No		Total	
		N	%	N	%	N	%
Police Doing							
a Good Job?	Yes	25	17	64	43	89	59
	No	51	34	10	6	61	41
	Total	76	51	74	49	150	100

Total percents are calculated here because it is difficult to determine just which variable is independent and which is dependent. The chi-square statistic is calculated as 44.3 with 1 degree of freedom (significant beyond the .001 level of error). The phi statistic indicates a moderately strong association of .54.

Lambda is calculated by:

Lambda (λ) = $f - m / N - m$

Where: f = sum of the largest cell frequencies with each attribute
            of the "independent" variable
      m = largest margin total among attributes of the
            "dependent" variable
      N = total number of observations or cases (sample size).

Using "fear of crime" as the independent variable, our largest cell frequencies are 51 respondents under the "Yes" attribute and 64 respondents under the "No" attribute. These two values are summed for the f in the formula. Using "police doing a good job" as the dependent variable, we find the largest marginal total (m) is 89. Plugging these values into the formula, we get:

λ = (51 + 64) – 89 / 150 – 89
    = 26 / 61
λ = .43

A lambda of .43 indicates that using "fear of crime" as the independent variable, we can predict how people feel about the police doing a good job with a 43 percent accuracy rate. Reversing the "independent" and "dependent" terms gives an indication as to which variable is a better predictor of the other. Now use "fear of crime" as the dependent variable and confidence in "police doing a good job" as the independent variable. Plugging the new values into the lambda formula, we get:

λ = (51 + 64) – 76 / 150 – 76
    = 39 / 74
λ = .53

A lambda of .53 indicates that opinions about how well the police are doing more accurately predicts fear of crime than fear of crime predicts opinions about how well the police are doing. In other words, if the public's opinions about the police were to change for the better, we would expect their fear of crime to diminish.

EXERCISES

Short-Answer Questions

One hundred jurors were polled on how well they understood instructions given to them by the judge. Their responses were collapsed and dichotomized into "understood" and "did not understand." Their verdicts in the jury trials were crosstabulated with their responses. The verdicts were dichotomized as "guilty" or "not guilty." Below are the data:

Total number of "guilty" verdicts = 60
Total number of "not guilty" verdicts = 40
Total number of jurors who "did not understand" = 40
Total number of jurors who "understood" = 60
Number of jurors who "understood" with "guilty" verdicts = 30
Number of jurors who "did not understand" with "guilty" verdicts = 30

1. Construct a 2 x 2 crosstabulation table for the data above. Include percents.

2. The independent variable is _____.

3. The dependent variable is _____.

4. Determine if jurors who do not understand jury instructions are more likely to vote "guilty." Calculate a chi-square statistic and provide a conclusion at the .05 level of significance.

5. Calculate a phi or Cramer's *V* correlation coefficient on the above data. What are your conclusions?

Multiple-Choice Questions

_____ 1. _____ presents frequencies and percentages in tabular format.

      a.   statistical analysis
      b.   table for research
      c.   contingency table analysis
      d.   none of the above

_____ 2. Contingency tables are _____ or more frequency distributions placed side by side.

      a.   2
      b.   3
      c.   4
      d.   5

_____ 3. An example of a nonparametric test is

      a.   contingency test
      b.   pie test
      c.   statistic test
      d.   chi-square

_____ 4. _____ and _____ are sample statistics.

      a.   mean, median
      b.   mean, standard deviation
      c.   standard deviation, variance
      d.   variance, chi square

_____ 5. Chi-square distributions are concerned with _____ and _____ data.

      a.   nominal, ordinal
      b.   interval, ratio
      c.   nominal, interval
      d.   ordinal, ratio

_____ 6. All chi-square tests involving a comparison or two variables are

      a.   directional
      b.   one-tailed
      c.   two-tailed
      d.   all of the above

_____ 7. Formula adjustment for small samples is called:

      a.   continuity adjustment
      b.   Yates's adjustment
      c.   Yates's Rule
      d.   Yates's Correction for Continuity

_____ 8. Another method to adjust for small samples involves:

      a.   extrapolating data
      b.   expanding data
      c.   collapsing data
      d.   none of the above

_____ 9. The key to collapsing data is finding two variables that

    a. are exhaustive
    b. logically go together
    c. are mutually exclusive
    d. do not logically go together

_____ 10. Strictly speaking, chi-square measures only the _____ of a relationship.

    a. dispersion
    b. variance
    c. significance
    d. *t* score

_____ 11. Contingency tables are useful for _____ level(s) of data.

    a. any
    b. 2
    c. 3
    d. 1

_____ 12. A statistic that measures the strength of a relationship is:

    a. *z* score
    b. *t* score
    c. chi-square
    d. phi

_____ 13. _____ measures the extent to which a value of one variable can be predicted from known values of other variables.

    a. lambda
    b. phi
    c. Cramer's *V*
    d. *z* score

_____ 14. For causation to exist, there must be:

    a. correlation
    b. temporal priority
    c. ruling out of competing explanations
    d. all of the above

True/False Questions

_____ 1. Correlation proves causation.

_____ 2. Correlation is one condition for establishing causation.

_____ 3. Contingency tables are simply two or more frequency distributions placed side by side.

_____ 4. Phi is the appropriate test of significance for a two-by-two contingency table.

_____ 5. Cramer's *V* is the appropriate test of significance for a contingency table with more than three columns or three rows.

_____ 6. Chi-square measures the strength of a relationship for data in a contingency table.

_____ 7. Yates's correction for continuity is used if a cell in a contingency table has too many cases.

_____ 8. If you wanted to compare some recidivism to no recidivism for parolees and offenders released from prison, a contingency table would be one effective way to examine the possible relationship.

_____ 9. If chi-square is statistically significant, phi will be significant.

_____ 10. If chi-square is statistically significant, Cramer's *V* will not be significant.

_____ 11. If phi is both significant and large, you can conclude with certainty that *X* causes *Y*.

Discussion/Essay Questions

1. Discuss when contingency tables are helpful in presenting data. When might they not be helpful?

2. How can lambda be useful in criminal justice practice? Give an example or make up a criminal justice situation where lambda could be used.

16

Deciding Which Statistical Test to Use

KEY TERMS

bivariate analysis
data transformation
decision tree
dependent variable
discriminant function analysis
factor analysis
hierarchical
independent variable
level of measurement
log linear analysis
multiple regression

multivariate analysis
nonparametric
null hypothesis
operationalization of variables
parametric
research hypothesis
skewness
stepwise
test of independence
test of relationship
test of significant difference

CHAPTER SUMMARY

I. Deciding Which Test to Use

A. When deciding which statistical test to use, there are a few important steps to take. First, you must define the hypothesis and variables. How many groups are there? What is the level of measurement? Are the samples normal? After these questions are answered, the appropriate test is chosen. This is not a monumental task, but it does take some time and thought. Go through the steps slowly and after the questions have been answered, choose which test is best suited to your project.

B. Selecting the appropriate statistical test to use with your research data is very important. In order to do this you must first understand the job that needs to be done.

II. Defining the Hypothesis to be Tested

Defining the hypothesis to be tested is the key to deciding what kind of study is being performed. If the hypothesis indicates that a test of difference between means needs to be conducted, you are looking to do a *t* test, analysis of variance or a nonparametric alternative. When a hypothesis suggests that a relationship exists between two variables, test for correlation by using Pearson's *r* or chi-square. After determining the hypothesis, the researcher must consider three questions.

A. *How many groups are in the sample or population?* The answer to this question will determine whether you need to run a one-sample test, a two-sample test, etc. If you have more than one group, how many times are they going to be measured? From here you can decide whether you need a one-sample test or a repeated-measures test.

B. *What is the level of measurement?* In order to answer this question, identify the dependent and independent variables and decide which level they fall under (nominal, ordinal, interval or ratio). If the variables are on the nominal or ordinal level, use a nonparametric test. If one variable is nominal and the other interval, use a parametric test. If both variables are at the interval level, then regression or correlation tests should be used.

C. *Are the samples normally distributed?* You can compare your sample to the normal distribution only if you are using a parametric test, a *t* test or a Pearson's *r* test. If your sample is large enough and the sample is taken from a normal population, you can reasonably assume that the data is normally distributed. Looking at the skewness of the population can help to determine whether the data are normal or not.

1. *Example:* Suppose we have a sample of test scores for women and a separate sample of scores for men. We want to compare the two samples. First, state a hypothesis (e.g., the test scores of women are higher than the test scores of men). The null hypothesis would state that there is no difference between men's and women's test scores. Next, determine the number of groups in the study (i.e., two). The independent variable is gender and the dependent variable is the test score. The level of measurement for the independent variable is nominal and the level of measurement for the dependent variable is ordinal; therefore, we must use a nonparametric test.

2. *Points to remember:* Parametric tests are typically considered stronger than nonparametric tests. The power of a test is determined by the ability to reject the null hypothesis. Therefore, always strive to obtain the highest level of measurement for your data as possible. Sometimes it is necessary to transform data to a higher level of measurement.

3. *Data Transformation:* In situations where there is a scale (e.g., strongly agree to strongly disagree), a researcher can assign a number to represent each answer, which then transforms the data into interval-level data rather than nominal data. Then we can apply a parametric test to the data rather than a nonparametric test. Transformations also can be made by multiplying or adding a number to each value in the data set or by squaring the values to eliminate negative numbers. In addition, transformations can be made when the data in a study do not meet the assumptions of normality or if the data in a correlation study have a curvilinear relationship (they can be transformed to make a more linear relationship).

III. Review: Parametric Tests

Parametric tests are used when the level of measurement is at least interval, and when the researcher can reasonably assume the data is normally distributed. When samples have 100 or more values, proportions of nominal data can be used (e.g., *z* tests).

One-Sample Means Tests

Hypothesis tested: H_o: μ = Standard mean selected by the researcher (two-tailed).

Research question: *Is there a significant difference between means?*

Number of groups: One group (population) or sample.

Level of measurement: Dependent variable at least interval. Means must be calculated. Independent variable—any level.

Use: When a mean of a sample or population is to be compared with some "standard" mean.

Tests and requirements: One-sample z test when sample numbers 100 or more. One-sample t test when sample numbers under 100.

Two-Sample Means Tests

Hypothesis tested: H_o: $\mu_1 = \mu_2$ (two-tailed).

Research question: *Is there a significant difference between means?*

Number of groups: Two groups with one measurement each (independent groups) or one group with two measures (matched group).

Level of measurement: Dependent variable at least interval. Means must be calculated. Independent variables—any level.

Use: When means for two samples or populations are to be compared (independent groups) or when two means from one group are to be compared (matched group).

Tests and requirements: Two-sample z test for independent samples when each of the samples or groups numbers 100 or more. Two-sample matched z test when the one sample or group numbers 100 or more. Two-sample t test for independent samples when each of the samples or groups numbers under 100. Two-sample matched t test when the one sample or group numbers under 100.

Two-Sample Proportion Tests

Hypothesis tested: H_o: $P_1 = P_2$ (two-tailed).

Research question: *Is there a significant difference between populations?*

Number of groups: Two groups with one measurement each (independent) or one group with two measures (matched).

Level of measurement: Dependent and independent variables—any level. Percents or proportions must be calculated.

Use:	When proportions or percents of two groups are to be compared (independent) or when two proportions from one group are to be compared (matched, commonly used when the independent variable cannot be readily identified).
Tests and requirements:	z test for proportions-independent groups: when each of the groups numbers 100 or more. z test for proportions—matched group: when the one group numbers 100 or more. For less than 100, see chi-square in the section on nonparametric tests.

Three or More (K) Sample Means Tests

Hypothesis tested:	H_o: $\mu_1 = \mu_2 = \mu_k$ (two-tailed only).
Research question:	*Are there significant differences among means?*
Number of groups:	Three or more groups with one measure each (independent) or three or more measures from one group (repeated measures).
Level of measurement:	Dependent variable at least interval. Means must be calculated. Independent variable—any level.
Use:	When means for three or more groups are to be compared (independent) or when means for three or more measures of one group are to be compared (repeated measures).
Tests and requirements:	One-way ANOVA when one independent variable is examined with dependent variable measures from three or more groups (there should be 30 or more subjects in each group or equal variances among the three groups). Repeated-measures ANOVA when one independent variable is examined with three or more dependent variable measures from one group (there should be 30 or more subjects for the group). Two-way and multiple-way ANOVA when two or more independent variables are being examined with dependent variable measures from three or more groups (there should be at least 30 or more subjects for each group, or there should be equal variances among the three or more groups). Multiple comparison procedures are used with ANOVA for examining *significant* differences between means. These procedures determine where the significant differences are between two or more means. Multiple comparison procedures can be used only with independent groups ANOVA. Two commonly used multiple comparison tests are the Scheffé test and Tukey's HSD test.

Tests of Relationship (Correlation and Regression)

Hypothesis tested:	H_o: $\rho_{xy} = 0$.
Research question:	*Is there a significant relationship between the independent variable (X) and the dependent variable (Y)?*
Number of groups:	One group or sample being examined on one or more independent variables.
Level of measurement:	Independent and dependent variables are measured at least on the interval level. Means must be calculated.

Use: When a causal relationship is thought to exist between the independent (*X*) variable and the dependent (*Y*) variable (correlation). Predicting values of the dependent variable (*Y*) from the existence of the independent (*X*) variable (regression).

Tests and requirements: Pearson's *r* for correlation (there should be at least 30 or more subjects in the group or sample). A linear (straight-line) relationship must be present. Partial correlation (partial *r*) is a correlation technique that controls for the effects of a third variable (*Z*) on the original correlation between *X* and *Y*. Regression analysis is used in conjunction with correlation to predict the change in the dependent variable (*Y*) based on a change in the independent variable (*X*). Multiple regression is used in conjunction with correlation to predict the change in the dependent variable (*Y*) based on changes of a number of independent variables (X_i).

IV. Nonparametric Tests

Nonparametric tests are generally used when the level of measurement is less than interval or if the sample or population is not normally distributed. Examples are the Mann-Whitney *U* test, the Wilcoxon test, chi-square, the Friedman ANOVA and the Kruskal-Wallis test.

V. Multivariate Techniques

More advanced tests such as multiple regression analysis, factor analysis, discriminant function analysis and log linear analysis are multivariate techniques.

EXERCISES

Multiple-Choice Questions

———— 1. Which of the following is the key to determining which statistical test to use?

   a. sample size
   b. hypothesis
   c. level of measurement
   d. all of the above

———— 2. If you are using a _____ test, data must be normally distributed.

   a. directional
   b. nondirectional
   c. parametric
   d. nonparametric

———— 3. Changing a set of data values from one measurement scale to another is called:

   a. coding
   b. multiplication
   c. data transformation
   d. number crunching

———— 4. The type of test used when the level of measurement is at least interval is:

   a. nonparametric
   b. one-tailed
   c. two-tailed
   d. parametric

———— 5. Pearson's r is a test of:

   a. relationship
   b. causation
   c. independence
   d. none of the above

———— 6. The test used when the level of measurement is less than interval is:

   a. parametric
   b. nonparametric
   c. directional
   d. nondirectional

———— 7. The test used when the dependent variable is *at least* ordinal and the independent variable is at any level is the:

   a. ANOVA
   b. Pearson's r
   c. z test
   d. Mann-Whitney U test

_____ 8. Which of the following is a correlation test?

    a. Spearman's rho
    b. Kendall's tau
    c. Goodman and Kruskal's gamma
    d. all of the above

_____ 9. Which test is *not* used to test associations between X and Y variables?

    a. Pearson's *r*
    b. Spearman's rho
    c. chi-square
    d. *t* test

_____ 10. A relationship between two variables is called a _____ relationship.

    a. bivariate
    b. multivariate
    c. bimodal
    d. unimodal

_____ 11. _____ allows researchers to select predictor variables assumed to be related to criterion variables.

    a. factor analysis
    b. multiple regression
    c. discriminant function analysis
    d. log linear analysis

_____ 12. Which of the following can be used as a data reduction technique?

    a. factor analysis
    b. multiple regression
    c. discriminant function analysis
    d. log linear analysis

_____ 13. _____ requires only nominal-level measurement.

    a. factor analysis
    b. multiple regression
    c. discriminant function analysis
    d. log linear analysis

_____ 14. A useful technique for exploratory studies involving large numbers of variables is:

    a. factor analysis
    b. multiple regression
    c. discriminant function
    d. log linear analysis

_____ 15. If you want to predict how many crimes an offender will commit after release from prison, based on a number of independent variables, the appropriate statistical test is:

    a. bivariate regression
    b. multiple regression
    c. correlation
    d. none of the above

True/False Questions

———— 1. If you measure recidivism (new crimes) dichotomously (success vs. failure), the appropriate statistical test to compare the recidivism of men vs. women offenders would be a t test.

———— 2. If you measure recidivism (new crimes) by the actual number of new crimes committed during the first year after an offender's release from prison, the appropriate statistical test to compare the recidivism of men vs. women offenders would be chi-square.

———— 3. If you want to predict how many crimes an offender will commit after release from prison based on a number of independent variables, the appropriate statistical test is bivariate regression.

———— 4. If you want to determine whether prior record (number of crimes committed prior to the current offense) is related to the number of crimes a person commits while he or she is on probation, the appropriate statistical test is Pearson's correlation coefficient (r).

———— 5. Three different reading programs are used on three different groups of prisoners. The appropriate statistical test to compare the reading scores (measured from 0 to 100 for each prisoner) at the end of the experiment is analysis of variance.

———— 6. Factor analysis is an appropriate way to determine which of 50 items measuring job satisfaction belong together because they are measuring a particular facet of job satisfaction.

———— 7. Correlation proves causation.

———— 8. A statistical test that allows one to examine the effects of many independent variables is multiple regression.

Essay/Discussion Questions

1. For each of the following determine the least required levels of measurement. Give an example for each.

   a. Pearson's r

   b. ANOVA

   c. lambda

   d. Wilcoxon

   e. discriminant function analysis

2. Assume you were planning to conduct a study of recidivism for probationers, offenders under electronic monitoring, and intensive supervision offenders in your state. Discuss how you would measure recidivism and what sorts of statistical tests would be most appropriate for your study.

_____

_____

_____

_____

_____

_____

_____

_____

_____

_____

_____

_____

_____

3. Assume you are about to study the job satisfaction of police officers on foot patrol compared to officers on car patrol. What sorts of measures would you use? What statistical tests might be most appropriate for your data analysis?

_____

_____

_____

_____

_____

_____

_____

_____

_____

_____

_____

_____

_____

17

Statistical Inference and Reporting

KEY TERMS

ethics
Humphreys's *Tearoom Trade* study
informed consent
Minnesota Domestic Violence Project

misconduct in science
refereed journal
Scared Straight documentary

CHAPTER SUMMARY

I. Ethics in Research

The primary goal of all science is to seek and report the truth. There are also a number of other important things to consider while seeking the truth, such as informing those people studied of what is going on and attempting to maintain an unbiased method and account of the research. Ethics are difficult to define, and it is often left up to the individual researcher to decide whether he or she is following the ethical guidelines properly. Unfortunately, some researchers do not seem to follow any guidelines.

A. Examples of dishonest research include fabrication, falsification and plagiarism.

B. Scientists use a "refereed" system in which a group of scientists reads the work without knowing who wrote it and decides whether it should be published. This ensures that a work is judged on its scientific merit.

C. One ethical issue is the question of whether and when it is appropriate for criminal justice researchers to seek publicity. Sherman conducted the Minneapolis Domestic Violence Project and found that arresting the suspect was the most effective response to domestic violence calls. This finding was publicized widely. The experiment was later replicated in Omaha, Nebraska, and Charlotte, North Carolina, with results that differed from those found in Minneapolis. These later findings suggested that the Minneapolis results were only tentative and needed further research. This raises the ethical issue of publicizing results prematurely, prior to adequate replication (repetition). Also exemplifying the publicity issue is the *Scared*

Straight documentary, which showed a group of youths who toured the Rahway State Prison in New Jersey. The documentary claimed that the experience scared the youths out of crime permanently. Publicity from this documentary implied that its effects were all positive, when in fact some youths who went through this type of program ended up worse than before, showing how widespread publicity about a study can be very misleading.

II. Topic Selection

A. *Personal values*: A researcher's own personal values may affect the way the research is carried out. Johnson's study of death row inmates illustrates what can happen. He presented the inmates in a sympathetic light, failing to expose the whole picture of death row inmates.

B. *Funding priorities:* When federal funding is obtained, researchers are often limited to topics related to a specific agenda. For example, the government has been very concerned with law enforcement issues to the exclusion of other criminological issues.

C. *Witnessing wrongdoing while researching:* Marquart had to deal with witnessing wrongdoing while conducting participant-observation research in a Texas prison. He witnessed guard brutality and had to weigh the possibility of having his research terminated against reporting the activity to authorities.

III. Informed Consent

The researcher is obligated to explain the study, as well as any possible risks, to potential subjects. The subjects must be capable of giving their authorization (consent) in a noncoerced environment. Problems can occur due to the following factors:

A. *Information about the study is not clear and complete:* Unless the subjects have such information, they cannot make an informed decision about participating.

B. *Nature of environment*: Consent of prisoners may never be completely voluntary due to the nature of the prison environment. Most observers agree that it is difficult for prisoners to give voluntary consent. Prisoners are likely to think that agreeing to participate in a research project may positively affect their chances for parole or early release.

C. *Effects of full disclosure:* The researcher must consider the effect of full disclosure to subjects in participant-observation studies. Humphreys's famous *Tearoom Trade* study illustrated that some studies are more successfully completed with covert techniques.

D. *Negative findings:* Negative findings in a study may be concealed if the researcher has a financial interest in the study.

IV. Undercover Research

Humphreys's *Tearoom Trade* study on the practices of homosexuals was criticized because the subjects did not realize they were being studied. Cassell also felt the subject was unscientific. Humphreys, however, did reveal his identity as a researcher to some of the subjects and, further, did adopt an actual role. The researcher has to weigh complete honesty against the possibility that such honesty may affect the behavior of subjects.

V. Truth in Report Writing

For truthful report writing, the following guidelines apply:

A. Give a complete description of the methodology so that the research can be replicated.

B. Inform readers of the limitations of the study.

C. Distinguish between the results of the research and the interpretation of the results.

VI. Kimmel's Guidelines for Ethical Research

A. Have a true concern for the subjects.

B. Weigh the costs and benefits of (1) doing the research; (2) not doing the research, and (3) doing the research another way.

C. Offer details on ethical procedures used.

D. The scientific community needs to monitor itself.

E. Scientists need to be aware of ethical trends in society and in the scientific community.

EXERCISES

Fill-in-the-Blank Questions

1. Examples of dishonest research are _____ and _____.

2. To ensure that a work is judged on its scientific merit, scientists use a _____ system.

3. The Minneapolis Domestic Violence Project was conducted by _____. It concluded that the best way to handle suspects was to _____ them. (counsel / arrest / remove).

4. Informing subjects completely of the study and getting their authorization is called _____ _____.

5. A complete description of the methodology of research is important so the research can be _____.

Multiple-Choice Questions

_____ 1. The primary _____ issue in criminal justice research is to seek and report the truth.

   a. empirical
   b. ethical
   c. criminal justice
   d. scientific

_____ 2. Fabrication, falsification or plagiarism in proposing, performing or reporting research is described as

   a. errors of judgment
   b. corrupt research
   c. empirical errors
   d. misconduct in science

_____ 3. Which of the following scientists have not been criticized for allegedly taking part in scientific misconduct?

   a. Freud
   b. Humphreys
   c. Cassell
   d. Sherman

_____ 4. Unethical procedures may include

   a. publicity-seeking
   b. biased topic selection
   c. predetermined findings
   d. all of the above

_____ 5. The Scared Straight program took place at which prison?

    a. Rahway (New Jersey)
    b. Attica (New York)
    c. Joliet (Illinois)
    d. Leavenworth (Kansas)

_____ 6. Personal values _____ affect topics of research but _____ the research.

    a. do, should clarify
    b. do, should not distort
    c. do not, should not distort
    d. do not, should motivate

_____ 7. Johnson did a study of

    a. school children
    b. elderly athletes
    c. death row inmates
    d. prison guards

_____ 8. _____ may dictate what topics are chosen to research.

    a. Funding
    b. Politics
    c. both a and b
    d. neither a nor b

_____ 9. When witnessing wrong doing, the researcher

    a. should go immediately to authorities
    b. may not go to authorities
    c. may continue research
    d. should weigh the pros and cons of informing authorities

_____ 10. Subjects should sign a voluntary _____ form.

    a. waiver
    b. tort contract
    c. consent review
    d. informed consent

_____ 11. The central purpose of research is

    a. seeking the truth
    b. obtaining funding
    c. earning tenure
    d. career advancement

_____ 12. Guidelines for truthful reporting do *not* include

    a. complete descriptions
    b. complete reporting
    c. unbiased opinions
    d. logical inferences

_____ 13. Kimmel gave some guidelines for ethical research. They do not include

        a. true concern for one's subjects
        b. awareness of ethical climate of the community
        c. monitoring
        d. maximizing publicity

True/False Questions

_____ 1. Arresting the suspect proved to be the most effective means of handling domestic violence calls in the Minneapolis domestic violence experiment.

_____ 2. Lempert has criticized Sherman for publicizing a preliminary finding from one study in such a way that suggested more importance to the findings than they deserved.

_____ 3. Arresting domestic violence suspects in Omaha, Nebraska, proved to be more effective in deterring domestic violence than other strategies.

_____ 4. Research has conclusively shown that most youths who have been exposed to prison tours and confrontation sessions have changed their lives drastically.

_____ 5. If the data support a conclusion contrary to the scientist's personal values, the scientist should report both the conclusion and the supporting data.

_____ 6. Johnson alleges that the way capital punishment is administered in the United States "strips prisoner and executioner alike of their humanity and is an actual, and not merely metaphorical, instance of torture."

_____ 7. One problem in seeking grant money to conduct research is that governmental funding agencies tend to fund research that promises immediate results.

_____ 8. In some observational studies (for example, the Stanford prison simulation and Black and Reiss's study of police), subjects were told that the scientists were interested in studying how others reacted to the subjects when in fact the scientists were very interested in the reactions of the subjects.

_____ 9. Humphreys's famous study of men engaging in homosexual behaviors at a public park restroom involved no disclosure of the researcher's identity or the nature of the study or even the fact that the subjects were under investigation.

_____ 10. Hirschi's study of junior and senior high school students lost only 1 percent of the original sample due either to parental refusal or failure to respond to the request for their consent.

_____ 11. Humphreys concealed his role as a researcher by acting as a "watch queen"; he watched for police while other men engaged in sexual contact in the restroom.

_____ 12. According to the text, all human behavior is worth studying. It is only after something is studied that we will have any idea what results might come out of the study.

_____ 13. According to the text, there is no perfect protection or safeguard against a scientist who wants to deceive.

_____ 14. According to Fine, researchers make choices and those choices are never perfect ethical choices.

Essay/Discussion Questions

1. Discuss what topics you would prefer *not* to research. Why do you feel that way?

2. How do you feel about disclosing your status as a researcher? When would you not disclose the fact that you are conducting research? What harm is there in not disclosing your status as a researcher?

3. Choose any study discussed in class or in the textbook and point out the ethical choices that the researcher made. Do you agree or disagree with those ethical choices? Why?

_____

_____

_____

_____

_____

_____

_____

_____

_____

_____

_____

_____

_____

_____

_____

_____

_____

_____

_____

_____

_____

_____

_____

_____

_____

_____

_____

_____

4. You are conducting a participant observation study. You are at a party and want to see how many people drink and drive. Should you tell the people at the party what you are doing? Why or why not? What other problems might you encounter in conducting this study?

5. Sherman has argued that it is appropriate to seek publicity for research findings. Do you agree or disagree? Discuss.

Appendix:
Case Study Problems

In this appendix we present some case study problems for analysis and discussion. We feel that research methods and statistics raise some important issues that merit extended discussion. We also feel that discussion is an important teaching and learning strategy. These case study problems can be used individually to reinforce learning or can be used as an integral component of in-class activity. The authors have broken their own classes into groups. The groups discussed case study examples and then reported their findings to the entire class.

Evaluation Research

Case Study 1

You have just been awarded a lucrative grant worth hundreds of thousands of dollars. With funds from the grant you will be able to devote two years to conduct research on a topic that you have been very eager to research for sometime. The grant will provide you with the time and the means to study what you really want to study.

Just before you are to begin work on your grant, you learn that the funding agency wants the results to come out a certain way. The agency wants to show that the new program you will be evaluating is successful in reducing crime. They will require interim reports every six months and if the first six-month report does not show results consistent with their preconceived notions, they will terminate the grant.

You do not really know what the results will be. Based on previous research, however, you have a strong basis for predicting that the new program will *not* be all that successful in reducing crime. Knowing that the funding agency wants positive findings no matter what, should you go to work on the grant or just quit now? What options do you have?

Survey Research

Case Study 2

You have just finished a two-year study of burglars. You directed a staff of five interviewers who went out and spent about three hours with 20 burglars each. You are scheduled to present the results of your study tomorrow at a national convention of criminologists. The media will be there to report on your findings. At 8:00 P.M. the evening before your presentation you learn that one of your interviewers "faked" her interviews; she fabricated all her data. A quick examination of the results of her interviews suggests to you that the faked interviews are very plausible. No one is likely to guess about the fabrication. Furthermore, the majority of the interviews (80 out of 100) were *not* faked, so your results are about 80 percent accurate.

What should you do?

Case Study 3

As a class project, design a survey that the class can administer to students in your department and/or your campus. Possible topics might be: attitudes toward capital punishment, attitudes toward building more prisons in your state, attitudes toward criminal justice occupations, victimization experiences, or self-reports of delinquent/criminal activity. Note, however, that victimization surveys and self-report surveys involve sensitive topics.

Be sure to discuss what topics should be included in the survey and why they are important. Also, discuss question wording and whether the class wants to use an interview approach or a self-administered questionnaire strategy.

Participant Observation

Case Study 4

You are conducting participant observation in a police department. After six months of research you discover that about one-fourth of the police officers are corrupt. They are taking bribes on a regular basis from drug dealers in exchange for leaving those dealers alone. The police arrest drug dealers who do not pay any bribes but ignore the ones who do pay them. As a result, cocaine and crack are readily available in the city and many high school youths seem to be getting addicted.

Your research plan specified a full 12 months of observation. If you inform on the officers now, your study will be terminated prematurely. You feel that keeping silent and continuing the study may cause some additional teenagers to become addicted and perhaps even die, but you also feel that continuing the study has several worthwhile objectives. For example, if you finish the study it will offer a detailed account of how and why corruption occurs, and could help prevent similar instances of corruption in other police departments. Thus, continuing the study could have greater beneficial results in the long run.

a. What should you do?
b. Does it make any difference if you learn that one of the teenagers who is in danger of becoming addicted is your nephew?
c. Does it make any difference if your research is for your doctoral dissertation? If you do not finish your research you will not get your Ph.D. degree and you will not be able to obtain employment as a college professor.

Ethical Reporting

Case Study 5

You have just finished a study of the death row experience. You interviewed death row inmates, death row guards, the families of prisoners on death row and the families of victims. Looking at all the information you have collected, you are thinking of omitting the information from the families of the victims of the offenders on death row. Several of those family members gave extremely graphic details of the murders of their relatives. Several also gave poignant accounts of the larger harm done by the murderers. For example, several children of the victims are having serious adjustment problems since their father or mother was killed. They cannot sleep and they are doing poorly in school.

You want to omit this information because you are opposed to capital punishment and feel that including such information may detract from your case. The other parts of your study offer strong reasons for opposing capital punishment. For example, you have found that the guards practice psychological brutality on the prisoners and frequently taunt the prisoners. The information from the families of the victims makes the offenders look very brutal, while the other information makes them look human (very victimized and traumatized. The state legislature will be having a new debate and vote on capital punishment in the near future that will decide the fate of capital punishment in your state for the next 10 years. You are afraid that the information about the relatives of the victims of the murderers will be used by capital punishment proponents to retain capital punishment in your state.

What should you do?

Case Study 6

A major academic publishing company has asked you to review a book manuscript. The manuscript is a study of the court system in a midwestern state. After reading the manuscript, you discover that something is terribly wrong. The statistical results seem impossible; they are very unexpected based on previous research. It so happens that the study is based on a data tape that you have access to. You use your computer and prove that the results presented in the manuscript are phony. It is very unlikely that anyone else would discover the errors, however, because only you and the author are familiar with both the topic of the study and the advanced statistical techniques used in the study.

a. What should you do?
b. Does it make any difference that the author is a friend of yours?
c. Does it make any difference that the author is dying of cancer and this study could make him famous?

Case Study 7

You are a college professor at Ivy Walls University. One of your doctoral students has just submitted her dissertation for final approval. You have just returned from Thailand where you spent the summer doing library research at a major Thai university.

Reading the final draft of the dissertation, you discover that the doctoral candidate plagiarized her dissertation from a Thai study that is over 20 years old. You are probably the only one who knows this. It is unlikely that anyone else would discover the plagiarism because so few American scholars study Thai journals or books.

If you report the plagiarism, the student will not graduate and will be expelled from Ivy Walls University. She probably would not be admitted to any other doctoral program in criminal justice or criminology. You have come to respect this woman because she comes from a deprived family background and has really struggled to begin a career teaching and conducting research as a college professor. She has begged you not to report her plagiarism. She assures you that if you keep silent she will not make any efforts to publish her dissertation after she graduates. She also has just been awarded a grant to do a study on delinquents and it promises to be a groundbreaking study that offers considerable promise for preventing delinquency.

What should you do?

Case Study 8

You are a student in introductory psychology. Your instructor administered a survey in class at the beginning of the semester. Later in the year you learn that the professor presented the results at a psychology conference. From what you have heard, the results he presented do not sound plausible. You discussed the study with 15 of your classmates. Based on your own response and the responses of your classmates, it seems impossible that the professor could have found what he claims he found.

a. What should you do?
b. Does it make any difference that you are taking another course from this professor? You earned a grade of "A" in the first course and could use another "A" to boost your average.
c. Does it make any difference that you really like this instructor? Does it make any difference that he is an effective teacher who gets students interested in psychology?

Research Topic Selection

Case Study 9

You are a new faculty member at Scenic View State University. You have almost a certain chance of obtaining a lucrative research grant to study prison overcrowding. Your state department of correction will be awarding the grant to see if prison dormitories are a feasible solution to the overcrowding problems in your state.

The difficulty is that you are not really interested in researching the pros and cons of prison dormitories. You are interested in prison life and the adjustment problems of prisoners. You feel that the state merely wants to justify a decision that they have already made to implement increased use of dormitories.

Both your chairperson and your dean are pressuring you to apply for the grant. They feel that it will bring prestige to your university if you are awarded the grant. In addition, the grant would bring in about $25,000 in indirect costs that the university could spend on new computers that are desperately needed. Furthermore, if you get the grant, it will all but guarantee that you receive tenure and promotion. You have not published very much in the past and if you do not get this particular grant you may be in danger of not earning tenure and promotion.

What should you do?

Research and the Community

Case Study 10

You are conducting a study of drug use on your campus. You have discovered that a certain number of students use drugs occasionally for recreational purposes. Some of the users are excellent students. Some are planning careers in law enforcement, the health professions, teaching and law.

The president of the university learns of your study. He calls you into his office and demands that you disclose the identities of the drug users on campus. He promises that he is interested only in offering substance abuse counseling services to these students.

Based on a past incident at your university, you suspect that the president is not completely honest. You are worried that he might send any information you give him to local police authorities for criminal prosecution.

a. What should you do?
b. Does it make any difference that the president knows you are in a particular fraternity and says that he is thinking of offering financial assistance for your fraternity's planned new house?
c. What steps could you have taken at the very beginning of your research to prevent such problems?

Statistical Analysis

The following case studies are designed to help you understand the nature of statistical decisionmaking. Often, students become so involved with the mechanics of statistics that they fail to understand the reasoning behind using statistics (Miller, 1988). As you react to the following cases and work the statistical problems, keep in mind what effects your decisions will have on the problem presented. Also, look for additional possible hypotheses that may provide an answer to your statistical findings.

Case Study 11

You are a lieutenant in the training division of a large police department. An assistant district attorney has requested a meeting with you regarding some police training she feels your officers need.

"Good morning," Assistant District Attorney Janet West exclaims as you enter her office.

"Morning, Janet. You say you need to discuss some training issues with me?," you ask while pulling a chair up to her desk.

"Well, I just wanted to mention some things that I feel may be a problem that you might be able to address in your training sessions," West responds.

"Over the past few months I've noticed that many of the officers have gotten a little sloppy in their case preparation for court and in their general courtroom demeanor," West states with a noticeable tone of concern in her voice.

"Gotten sloppy? What do you mean?," you ask with a puzzled expression.

"Well, for instance, just last week, Patrol Officer Jim Smith came to court on a DUI case. When he testified, his general demeanor was of nonconcern and impatience. He was disorganized, he had forgotten his notes on the case and he even forgot to bring the Breathalyzer results. As a result of his lack of preparedness, the case was dismissed."

"I'll have his supervisor talk to him about it," you respond.

"Well, I don't think that's going to do it. Jim is just one example. I've seen it with many of the officers over the past few months. I think some in-service training on courtroom demeanor and case preparation is needed," West exclaims.

"You said all this started a few months ago?," you ask.

"Well, yeah. Most of the officers were very good in court up until about four months ago. I've also noticed a decline in the numbers of arrests they're making. Maybe they're getting burned out or something," West responds.

Leaving West's office you realize that there is a problem. Something has occurred to make your officers less enthusiastic about going to court and making arrests. You decide to review your department's policy and procedures changes for the last year to see if any change in policy may have affected your officers' behavior. You also request the Records Bureau to send you copies of arrest and conviction reports for the last year.

Reviewing policy and procedures changes over the past year, you find a policy change regarding overtime pay for court appearances:

Effective immediately, all overtime pay for court appearances is limited to two hours per week regardless of the amount of time spent in court.

The new policy went into effect about four months ago. The department, in an effort to save money, decided to limit overtime pay for court appearances to two hours per week. The policy was implemented because a few officers were taking advantage of overtime pay for court appearances. You remember hearing some of the officers complaining about having to spend nearly all day in court and receiving only two hours overtime pay.

You found no other policy changes that could account for Janet West's observations. Is it possible that officers, reacting to the two-hour limit on court overtime pay, were not being as aggressive in their arrest procedures and spending less time on case preparations for court?

Case Study 11—*continued*

To explore that feasibility, you sample 10 officers' records of arrest data before the implementation of the new policy, and compare this with arrest data after implementation of the new policy. Below are your data:

Officer	Mean Monthly Arrests Before Policy	Mean Monthly Arrests After Policy
1	21	16
2	31	20
3	25	12
4	18	9
5	7	8
6	14	13
7	16	8
8	23	11
9	19	8
10	12	6

Do you have evidence to indicate the new policy has decreased the number of arrests by your officers? Should the training division begin in-service training on courtroom demeanor and case preparation or should this matter be brought to the attention of the chief? Formulate the hypotheses, select the appropriate statistical test(s) and calculate the results. State what statistical test(s) you selected and why.

Case Study 12

You are a Child Protective Services worker with the Department of Human Services. Your primary job is to investigate allegations of child physical and sexual abuse. Over the years, you have noticed an increase in the numbers of reported incidents of child sexual abuse, particularly incest.

One of the characteristics of incestuous families you have observed is the educational level of the perpetrator. Incest perpetrators generally have lower educational levels than nonperpetrators. However, over the past few months that characteristic seems to have changed. It appears that there has been an increase in reported incidents of incest among higher-educated families. Your immediate reaction to this is that the increase is due to the depressed economy of the area.

Over the past year, several industries have laid off workers or closed down operations in your region. This has resulted in a higher than normal unemployment rate for your area. Since workers with college and even advanced graduate degrees have been affected, you feel it is unemployment rather than educational level that is related to the increased incidents of reported incest. You decide to investigate further.

You obtain the monthly unemployment rates for the year in your region, along with monthly reports of incest allegations. Below are your data:

Month	Unemployment Rate	Reports of Incest
1	6.1	3
2	6.3	3
3	6.1	4
4	7.4	5
5	7.0	4
6	7.6	5
7	7.7	6
8	8.1	7
9	8.9	7
10	8.4	7
11	9.0	8
12	8.6	9

Do you have evidence to indicate that the unemployment rate is related to reports of incest? If there is a significant relationship, why do you think an increase in unemployment would be related to an increase in the reports of incest? Formulate the hypotheses, select the appropriate statistical test(s) and calculate the results. State the statistical test(s) you selected and why.

Case Study 13

You are an Assistant District Attorney. Your primary responsibilities include prosecuting misdemeanor offenses and preliminary hearings for felony cases. You are also charged with the responsibility of supervising the clerical and support staff at the District Attorney General's Office. You are scheduled to meet with the District Attorney General this morning to discuss some issues about routine office matters.

"Come on in and grab a cup of coffee," District Attorney General Roger Lewis states with a grin.

"Thanks, Roger," you state, realizing that you probably look a little sleepy to Lewis.

"I've got one big favor I need you to work on. The news media is questioning me on the numbers of plea bargains that we have engaged in over the past several months. They're on this racial and poverty discrimination thing and they're trying to show that our plea bargaining arrangements are biased against minorities and the poor."

"That's ridiculous, Roger," you interrupt. "We've never been accused of discrimination when it comes to prosecutions."

"Now don't get too upset about this. You and I both know that we're not discriminating, but the statistics speak for themselves and they don't look good on this," Lewis says in a calming voice.

"A news reporter has obtained conviction statistics from the court clerk's office and it does look like we're convicting more minorities and poor people than affluent whites," Lewis states, handing you the court clerk's computer printout.

The statistics Lewis has handed you do reflect a possible bias. It seems that on cases that were plea bargained, a disproportionate number were minorities or poor.

"Well, this doesn't mean anything. It just says these people couldn't afford to hire a good lawyer and instead used the public defender's office. Everyone knows the public defender's office wants to plea out these cases," you answer, thumbing through the printout.

"Exactly," Lewis exclaims. "That's the favor I want of you. Everyone doesn't know this, except those of us in criminal justice. I want the news media to understand that the public defender's office is plea bargaining many of these cases out rather than going to trial. Here, look at the cases we've gone to trial with the past year." Lewis hands you yet another computer printout.

The printout shows all the jury trials in criminal court for the past year, the judge presiding in each case, the defense attorney, the prosecuting attorney and the verdict. The summary is as follows:

Total number of trials = 315
Total number of "guilty" verdicts = 206
Total number of "not guilty" verdicts = 104
Total number of hung juries = 5
Total number of cases defended by a public defender = 178
Total number of cases defended by a private attorney = 137
Number of cases defended by a private attorney ending in a "guilty" verdict = 73
Number of cases defended by a private attorney ending in a hung jury = 4
Number of cases defended by a public defender ending in a "guilty" verdict = 133

"It looks like if you can afford a private attorney you have a better chance of getting an acquittal or at least a hung jury," you remark.

"That's what I want you to look at. See if there's a significant relationship between type of defense attorney (whether a private paid attorney or a public defender) and the verdict (guilty, not guilty or hung jury)," Lewis answers.

"The public defender's office is not going to like it if that's the case," you comment.

"That's their problem. Let them handle the heat from the news media for a change," Lewis states with a smirk.

Case Study 13—*continued*

Do you have evidence to believe that there is a relationship between the type of defense attorney a defendant has (private attorney vs. public defender) and verdict (guilty, not guilty or hung jury)? Formulate the hypotheses, select the appropriate statistical test(s) and calculate the results. State the statistical test(s) you used and why.

Case Study 14

You are a captain with a medium-sized county sheriff's department. Your primary responsibilities include supervision of jail personnel and making policy for the county jail. A few months ago, the state supreme court ruled in favor of a class action suit filed by inmates in your jail that the county jail was overcrowded. The court mandated that the county had six months to alleviate the overcrowded conditions.

The county commission authorized funds to increase the size of the county jail by 75 beds in order to comply with the court's order. Delays in construction and the usual bureaucratic hassles with budget and jail design approval have left the county facing the court's deadline without meeting its order. One of the judges has informally advised the Sheriff that an extension is out of the question.

Sheriff Patterson approaches you with the problem.

"The county commission has put this thing in our lap and it looks as though we're going to have to do something before the court's deadline," says Patterson.

"But, Sheriff, we only have three months to do something. If the commissioners had acted on this sooner, we could."

"I know, I know," Patterson interrupts. "It's not the county commissioners that are going to look bad, it's going to be us. I want you to find a way we can alleviate the overcrowding in the jail prior to the deadline. I know that anything we do is only temporary, but it will get the courts off our backs and the ball back into the commissioners' court, so to speak," the Sheriff adds (pun intended).

Sheriff Patterson has left you with a big problem. You must find a way to significantly reduce the inmate population of your jail without increasing the number of beds.

Your jail is populated by mostly misdemeanor offenders. In fact, the average monthly percentage breakdown is:

State (felony) prisoners awaiting trial	=	20%
DUI offenders	=	25%
Other misdemeanors serving time	=	25%
Felons awaiting transfer to prison	=	10%
Public drunk/disorderly	=	15%
Mental patients awaiting transfer	=	5%

The largest group in the jail population is DUI offenders. A state law mandating jail time for DUI offenders has been the main problem creating the overcrowded conditions at your jail. There is little that can be done about that group of offenders. However, there is a state law that allows officers to issue citations in lieu of arrest for minor misdemeanor offenders (i.e., shoplifting, larceny, simple assault, etc.). It has not been your department's policy to issue citations in lieu of arrest for jailable offenses. However, if your officers began issuing citations in lieu of arrest, it might be the key to alleviating, at least temporarily, the overcrowded conditions at the jail.

You obtain the jail records for the past two years to determine what percentage of the jail population includes misdemeanor inmates awaiting trial that could be cited into court rather than stay in jail until their hearing. You find most of the misdemeanor offenders who stay in jail awaiting trial cannot afford bail. Many of those could have been cited rather than arrested and booked. The question is: Would such a policy alleviate the overcrowded conditions significantly enough to allow the jail to comply with the court order?

The court has indicated that a maximum average of 175 inmates a month can be held in your county jail. According to records for the last two years, an average of 209 inmates has been housed in the jail each month. You assume that the last two years are fairly representative of normal jail populations and can be used to predict future monthly jail populations. Examining the records, you remove those offenders that could have been cited rather than arrested and booked into jail. You prepare a listing of the actual jail population for the last 24 months and compare it with the jail population had citations been issued in lieu of arrest. Below are your data:

Case Study 14—*continued*

Month	Actual Jail Population	Jail Population with Citation Policy
1	209	187
2	208	189
3	201	181
4	230	191
5	241	207
6	233	201
7	201	188
8	200	176
9	180	164
10	195	152
11	215	171
12	210	173
13	210	158
14	201	143
15	209	188
16	208	191
17	195	166
18	216	191
19	219	190
20	221	184
21	198	177
22	199	179
23	210	183
24	214	186

Using the last two years data, would a citation in lieu of arrest policy *significantly* reduce the average number of inmates per month? Would a citation in lieu of arrest policy reduce the average number of inmates enough to comply with the court order of an average of 175 per month? Formulate the hypotheses and calculate the appropriate statistical test(s). State the statistical test(s) you used and why.

Case Study 15

Suppose Judge Parsons has given the following sentences (in months) to 10 defendants convicted of felonious assault: 12, 13, 15, 19, 26, 27, 29, 31, 40 and 48. There is nothing unreasonable about the average sentence of 26 months for felonious assault, but why did some receive 12 months and others receive as much as 48 months for the same offense? It could be prior record, defendant's race or even the judge's mood. Below are the sentences along with each offender's prior record and race:

Race (W = white N = nonwhite)	Priors	Sentence Received
N	0	12
W	3	13
W	1	15
W	0	19
N	6	26
W	5	27
N	3	29
W	4	31
N	10	40
W	8	48

Is there evidence to indicate that nonwhite offenders received harsher sentences than white offenders? Is there a significant relationship between prior convictions and sentence received for felonious assault? What sentence would a nonwhite offender likely receive if convicted of felonious assault with five prior convictions? Formulate the hypotheses and calculate the appropriate statistical test(s). State what statistical test(s) you used and why.

Case Study 16

You are a planning and research officer with a medium-sized police department. One of your duties is to prepare Uniform Crime Report data.

"We've got a problem," Deputy Chief Trexler states abruptly as she enters your office.

"What's up, Chief?," you ask, not really wanting to know.

"You know the city commission meeting is tomorrow night. We're presenting our next year's budget request. We're asking for a substantial increase in funds for our crime prevention program and our criminal investigations division."

"Yes, I know. I prepared some data to distribute among the commissioners. I haven't gotten it out to them yet, but . . ."

"Well, put a hold on that report," Trexler interrupts. "At least until we've strengthened our position. It seems that Commissioner Bailey has a copy of the UCR reports for the last two years and it shows very clearly that our crime prevention program and our criminal investigations division are doing worse rather than better."

"Worse? That's a crock," you state angrily. "We've actually done much better. I know the reports Bailey has and they show we've increased clearance rates on burglaries by six percent," you add.

"I know, but Bailey is referring to the amount of stolen property recovered in dollar amounts. The first year we recovered $270,500 in stolen property and the last year we recovered only $74,600 in stolen property. Those are the figures he is using against us," says Trexler.

Chief Trexler is right. According to your own UCR data, there were nine solved break-and-enters (B & Es) the first year, resulting in $270,500 recovered in stolen property (a mean of $30,056) and last year there were 13 solved B & Es, resulting in $74,600 in recovered stolen property (a mean of $5,738).

"Well, I can explain that right away. We recovered more property the first year because we solved that break-in at the road construction site. Remember they stole a bulldozer worth nearly $150,000; and then there was that break-in at that dental clinic where they stole more than $60,000 worth of gold. We recovered those two and . . ."

"I remember," Trexler interrupts again, "but the fact is that Bailey is going to harp on this recovered property thing in order to shoot us down on a budget increase. You know how he's been in the past in supporting the police department."

"Yeah, I know. He's not been what you call a friend of the department. I still think he's mad because we threw his brother in jail for public drunkenness a couple of years ago," you state.

"Well, anyway. Here's what I need from you. Get out a new report comparing the first year figures with the last year figures on stolen property recovered. Somehow you need to control for that bulldozer and that dental gold and show that we've actually done better. I'm no statistician, but even I know there's a significant difference between average recovered stolen property amounts of $30,000 and $6,000. The bulldozer and gold amounts are what you statisticians call . . . what is that term?"

"Skewed," you answer.

"Yeah, that's it, screwed. And that's what will happen to us if Commissioner Bailey has his way," Trexler comments. "If you can get me a new report by this afternoon, I'll get it to the newspaper and get a news feature on how well we're doing with our crime prevention program and criminal investigations. That should nullify any negative comments Bailey makes at the budget hearings. With a news report that states we're doing a good job, he'll look bad if he tries to downgrade our efforts," Trexler adds.

As Trexler leaves your office, you begin to look over the first and last year's B & E recovered stolen property data:

Case Study 16—*continued*

First Year Stolen Property Recovered ($)	Last Year Stolen Property Recovered ($)
142,000	16,000
62,000	15,000
16,000	11,000
11,500	8,000
11,000	6,000
9,000	4,000
8,000	4,000
7,000	3,000
4,000	2,000
	2,000
	1,600
	1,000
	1,000

a. What statistical procedure(s) can you use to show that your department has actually performed better that last year in comparison to the first year in recovered stolen property? State why you selected the statistical procedure(s).
b. State the hypotheses, calculate the appropriate statistical procedure(s) and report your findings.
c. Is there evidence to indicate that your department is doing better in recovered stolen property?

Case Study 17

You are a regional director for the state Department of Correction, Adult Probation Division. Your job consists of administrative tasks and the supervision of adult probation offices in six counties. One day you receive a telephone call from a newspaper reporter.

"Hello. This is John Schmidt with the Daily News in Midville. How are you today?"

"Fine," you answer apprehensively. You have always been very cautious when talking with newspaper reporters. You learned the hard way that everything you say can wind up in print, sometimes out of context.

"Just a couple of questions, Director. We're doing a story about disparity in sentencing and would like your opinions and some information as to the obvious sexual differences in handing out probation sentences."

"Sexual disparity?," you question.

"Yes. We've done some checking around on the sentences received in Davis County by Judge Hilton and found that a disproportionate number of female offenders are given probation rather than jail time like male offenders."

It becomes all too apparent to you now. Judge Hilton was recently accused of sexual harassment of female offenders. It seems he was accused of offering certain female offenders a more lenient probation sentence in return for sexual favors. The reporter is trying to get more information against Judge Hilton for another newspaper attack on the judge's character.

"Well, I don't know anything about disparity in sentencing. Sentences are the responsibility of the judge, not the probation office," you state, trying to steer clear of the controversy.

"Yes, I know. The judge's office suggested I contact you people to get the statistics on the number of probation sentences given for males and females in Hilton's court. They say it's your office that recommends sentences based on . . . I believe they called it a presentence report?"

"A presentence investigation report or PSI. But, no, we don't recommend a sentence. That's against our state law. All we do is prepare a report reflecting the background of the defendant. Such things as drug use, prior convictions, juvenile record and so on," you explain.

"Well, that would be great information to have," Schmidt states.

"I'm not at liberty to release any . . ."

"Not to worry, Director," Schmidt interrupts. "I've got the names of 30 defendants randomly selected from convictions in Judge Hilton's court. It is public information, you know. All I need from you is a brief summary of those things you just mentioned that influence a judge's decision to sentence jail or probation for these 30 offenders. I have clearance from your state commissioner. Like I said, this is public information according to state law."

You explain to Schmidt that you would try to obtain the information he requested. A phone call to the state commissioner's office verified that Schmidt was telling the truth about getting permission to examine PSI records for his 30 offenders.

You pull the computer records of PSIs for the 30 probationers that Schmidt randomly selected. They were all misdemeanor property offenses. They were equally divided between 15 males and 15 females. In your examination of the 30 offenders, you did not notice any particular difference between the males and the females with regard to prior convictions, drug use or juvenile record. However, the printouts did show one item that seemed to catch your eye. The PSI reports show whether the defendant pleaded guilty or not guilty to their offense in court. You notice that all but one of the female offenders pleaded guilty while only nine of the 15 males pleaded guilty. Below are the data from the printouts:

Case Study 17—*continued*

Offender	Sex	Priors	Drugs	Juv. Rec.	Plead Guilty
1	M	Yes	Yes	No	No
2	M	No	Yes	Yes	No
3	M	Yes	No	Yes	No
4	M	No	Yes	No	Yes
5	M	Yes	Yes	Yes	Yes
6	F	Yes	Yes	No	Yes
7	F	No	Yes	No	Yes
8	F	No	No	Yes	Yes
9	F	No	Yes	Yes	Yes
10	F	Yes	Yes	Yes	Yes
11	M	Yes	Yes	No	No
12	M	No	Yes	Yes	No
13	M	Yes	No	Yes	No
14	M	No	Yes	No	Yes
15	M	Yes	Yes	Yes	Yes
16	F	Yes	Yes	No	Yes
17	F	No	Yes	No	Yes
18	F	No	No	Yes	Yes
19	F	No	No	Yes	Yes
20	F	Yes	Yes	Yes	Yes
21	M	Yes	Yes	No	No
22	M	No	Yes	Yes	No
23	M	Yes	No	Yes	No
24	M	No	Yes	No	Yes
25	M	Yes	Yes	Yes	Yes
26	F	Yes	Yes	No	Yes
27	F	No	Yes	No	Yes
28	F	No	No	Yes	Yes
29	F	No	No	Yes	Yes
30	F	Yes	Yes	Yes	No

You wonder if there is a significant relationship between offender's sex and their pleading guilty or not guilty. If there was, it would certainly add fuel to the fire against Judge Hilton. On the other hand, recommendations for leniency usually comes from the prosecuting attorney's office. If there were a significant relationship between sex and pleadings it might unfairly damage Judge Hilton's character even further. This is especially true if Judge Hilton is innocent of sexual harassment. However, you did not mention to Schmidt the fact that PSIs have information about whether the defendant pleaded guilty or not guilty. Your only responsibility to the press is to provide information regarding the factors that help a judge render an appropriate sentence (prior convictions, drug use and juvenile record). If there were no significant differences between the 30 offenders based on these criteria and gender, the press would probably not be interested, since it would indicate that Judge Hilton is just doing his job. Perhaps you should omit the information about the defendant's plea. Schmidt could find this information from some other source (like the prosecuting attorney's office) and you would be out of the middle of any controversy. On the other hand, if Judge Hilton is sexually harassing female offenders in return for a lenient sentence of probation rather than jail time, maybe you should provide this information to the press. You strain to think it over.

Case Study 17—*continued*

a. Determine if there is a significant relationship between sex and pleadings.
b. Determine if there are significant relationships between sex and the other criteria (priors, drugs, juvenile record).
c. State the hypotheses and the statistical test(s) you used and why.
d. Should you release the information regarding the pleadings of the 30 offenders to the press? Defend your position.
e. What other data could you use to determine if there were significant relationships between gender and sentence received?

Reference

Miller, L.S. and M.C. Braswell (1988). "Teaching Criminal Justice Research: An Experiential Model." *American Journal of Criminal Justice XIII* (1), 26-39.

Criminal justice research and statistics involve a certain amount of mathematical calculation. As some readers may have had less exposure to mathematics than others, this pull-out review guide serves as a refresher on some mathematical basics that may have been forgotten.

Expressing Multiplication and Division Equations

Mathematical operations can be expressed in several ways. While most are familiar with the traditional multiplication (x) and division (÷) symbols, there are other ways to express multiplication and division equations.

For instance, to express the multiplication of X and Y, one could use any of the following formats:

$$X \times Y \qquad\qquad X \cdot Y$$

$$X(Y) \qquad\qquad X \cdot Y$$

$$XY \qquad\qquad (X)(Y)$$

Similarly, division can be expressed in more than one way. To divide X by Y, one could use any of the following expressions:

$$X \div Y$$

$$X / Y$$

$$\frac{X}{Y}$$

In a division equation, the number that appears first (or above the division line) is called the "numerator." The numerator is the number that is being divided. The number that appears second (or below the division line) is called the "denominator." The denominator acts as the divisor of the numerator.

Squares and Square Roots

Squares and square roots are operations frequently utilized in statistical operations. To square a number means to multiply it by itself. For example, 4^2 (four squared) = $4 \times 4 = 16$. Conversely, the square root of a number is the value that, when multiplied by itself, results in the original number. Therefore, $\sqrt{16}$ (the square root of sixteen) = 4.

Factorials

A factorial, symbolized by an exclamation point symbol (!), is the product of all the positive integers from 1 to n. For example, to compute the factorial of 4, one would multiply the integers 1 through 4. The equation would be as follows: $4! = 1 \times 2 \times 3 \times 4 = 24$.

Rounding

Often in statistical calculations the numbers used are carried out to several decimal places. A way to make such numbers manageable is to use rounding to the nearest decimal place. To round off, one needs to look at the digit immediately to the right of the final digit that will appear. If the digit is less than 5, round down; if it is 5 or greater than 5, round up. Therefore, the number 23.321 would be rounded to 23.32 if one were rounding off to the nearest 100ths place, to 23.3 if one were rounding off to the nearest tenths place, and to 23 if one were rounding off to the nearest whole number. [Note: In statistics, rounding off to whole numbers is not recommended.] The number 23.778 would be rounded to 23.78 at the nearest hundredths place and 23.8 at the nearest tenths place.

see other side

Summations

The Greek letter Σ (capital sigma) is used to symbolize the summation of a set of numbers. If X has the values 5, 8, 10, 13 and 15, then $\Sigma X = 5 + 8 + 10 + 13 + 15 = 51$.

How to Calculate a Mathematical Operation

The order in which a mathematical operation is completed can affect the accuracy of the results. The basic rules of precedence are to find all the squares and square roots first, then perform all multiplication and division tasks, and then complete any addition and subtraction. These rules of precedence, however, are overridden by any parentheses or brackets in an equation. When there are parentheses or brackets, the operation should be worked "from the inside out," meaning that any operation enclosed in parentheses or brackets should be completed first before going on to other operations in the equation.

For instance, $(5 + 6) \times 3$ should be worked out as follows. First, calculate the value for the equation within the parentheses: $5 + 6 = 11$. Then, insert the value of 11 in the equation to obtain: $11 \times 3 = 33$.

Understanding this process is invaluable as mathematical equations become more complex, as they often do in statistical calculations.

To solve the following equation:

$$\sqrt{\frac{(31 \times 151.3) + [30 \times (121.12 + 3)]}{31 + 30}}$$

First perform the operations in the parentheses:

$31 \times 151.3 = 4{,}690.3$

$121.12 + 3 = 124.12$

Then insert these values into the equation:

$$\sqrt{\frac{4{,}690.3 + [30 \times 124.12]}{31 + 30}}$$

Then perform the operation in brackets:

$30 \times 124.12 = 3{,}723.6$

Then insert the value obtained into the equation:

$$\sqrt{\frac{4{,}690.3 + 3{,}723.6}{31 + 30}}$$

Then add the values in the numerator and denominator

$$\sqrt{\frac{8{,}413.9}{61}}$$

Then complete the division problem within the square root symbol:

$8{,}413.9 \div 61 = 137.93278$

Then, compute the square root of that value: $\sqrt{137.93278} = 11.744478$ (rounded off to 11.74).